BOOK OF MORE NEW ZEALAND JOKES

John Barnett and Lesley Kaiser live in Auckland. They have been interested in jokes for a number of years. They are the compilers of *Shark-infested Custard*, and, with Brian Schaab, of *The Penguin Book of New Zealand Jokes*.

John Stoupe's parents came from Belfast, and he now lives in Whangarei. He served an apprenticeship as a carpenter and joiner in the 1940s, and was a taxi driver for 35 years. He has played many a good game of golf. John Stoupe is married with three children. 'Life,' he says, 'is full of humour and tragedy, and we are required to do our best with both.'

THE PENGUIN BOOK OF MORE NEW ZEALAND JOKES

Compiled by John Barnett
and Lesley Kaiser
in association with John Stoupe

PENGUIN BOOKS

PENGUIN BOOKS
Penguin Books (NZ) Ltd, Cnr Rosedale and Airborne Roads, Albany, Auckland 1310, New Zealand
Penguin Books Ltd, 27 Wrights Lane, London W8 5TZ, England
Penguin USA, 375 Hudson Street, New York, NY 10014, United States
Penguin Books Australia Ltd, 487 Maroondah Highway, Ringwood, Australia 3134
Penguin Books Canada Ltd, 10 Alcorn Avenue, Toronto, Ontario, Canada M4V 3B2
Penguin Books Ltd, Registered Offices: Harmondsworth, Middlesex, England

First published by Penguin Books (NZ) Ltd, 1998

1 3 5 7 9 10 8 6 4 2

Editorial services by Michael Gifkins
Designed and typeset by Egan-Reid Ltd
Printed in Australia by Australian Print Group, Maryborough

Damn braces, bless relaxes.
—William Blake

It's not if you win or lose, it's what you wear.
—Cyndi Lauper

CONTENTS

INTRODUCTION

This book is comprised of jokes that we collected in the two years after *The Penguin Book of New Zealand Jokes* was published. As with that title, which was compiled in association with Brian Schaab, it also includes the input of another joke collector, John Stoupe. Over the time it took to compile this book, we noted the development of new genres, the burgeoning of gay humour and, particularly of interest to those south of the Bombay Hills, the development of the anti-Auckland joke, fuelled no doubt by the Auckland power crisis. It's good to see that jokes keep on doing what they do, which is to burst forth, flourish, wane, transmute and then emerge refreshed by circumstance . . .

There's more humour available on Internet than ever before, and New Zealanders are increasingly availing themselves of those resources, finding, among other things, material that is locally pertinent. We note too the ever-increasing use of e-mail and photocopying of e-mail as a method of joke circulation.

Have a read, and have a laugh, and, whatever, remember that laughter is good for your health.

John Barnett and *Lesley Kaiser*

STARTERS

How do you know when there's an Egyptian at your door?
He'll toot and come in.

How do you make a sandwich spread?
Sit on it.

How can you identify a happy cyclist?
He has bugs in his teeth.

How do you cut the sea?
With a sea saw.

How do you start a pudding race?
Sago.

How many sides does a box have?
Two. The inside and the outside.

How do you make a Mexican chilli?
Take him to the North Pole.

How does the sea say hello?
It gives a little wave.

How do you keep a fool in suspense?
I'll tell you next week.

Where do you weigh a pie?
Somewhere over the rainbow.
[—I don't get it.]
Somewhere over the rainbow, way up high (weigh a pie).

How do you pronounce 'ghoti'?
Fish. ('Gh' as in rou*gh*; 'o' as in sec*o*nd; and 'ti' as in sta*ti*on.)

o o o

What is a bra?
An over-shoulder boulder holder.

What's purple, sweet and extremely large?
Moby Grape.

What type of boots do koalas wear?
Gum boots.

What's green and red and shaped like an olive?
An olive.

What's purple and lives in the ocean?
Grape Britain.

What's the most dangerous piece in a car?
The nut behind the wheel.

What's the definition of an economist?
Someone who marries Elle Macpherson for her money.

What have Winnie the Pooh and John the Baptist got in common?
The.

What do you give a girl who has everything?
A tube of penicillin, gift wrapped.

What is greeny-yellow, covered in custard and very, very unhappy?
Apple grumble.

What do robbers eat?
Take-away food.

What do you call an armless, legless pianist?
A clever dick.

o o o

What's black and blue and red all over?
A baby combing its hair with a potato peeler.

What did the zoo-keeper say to the children?
'I've got good gnus and bad gnus.'

What did one wall say to the other wall?
'Meet you at the corner.'

What game do you play on a wet billiards table?
Pool.

What do you call a boomerang that doesn't come back?
A stick.

What is the best exercise for losing weight?
Pushing yourself away from the table.

What did Michael Jackson say to his Barbie doll?
'You are not alone. I am plastic too.'

What did the wave say to the sand?
Nothing. It just waved.

What did the little strawberry say to the big strawberry?
'If it wasn't for you, I wouldn't be in this jam.'

What do you call three holes in the ground?
Well, well, well.

What job do hippies do?
They hold up your leggies.

What's French, yellow and swims underwater?
Jacques Custard.

What did the circus owner say to the human cannonball when the human cannonball resigned from the circus?
'I don't know where I'm going to get another man of your calibre.'

What lies at the bottom of the sea and whimpers?
A nervous wreck.

What's a barbecue?
A line of people waiting for a haircut.

What was Anne Boleyn's last meal?
Two cold chops.

What's a specimen?
An Italian astronaut.

What's a lawyer's favourite desert?
Sue-it pudding.

What kind of hair gives you a shock?
One white hair among the black.

What's round and violent?
A vicious circle.

What's worse than finding a worm in an apple?
Finding half a worm.

What were Tarzan's last words?
'Who greased the viiiiiiiiiiiiiiine?'

What does divine mean?
It's what de grapes grow on.

What's white with wings?
An angel.

What's black with wings?
A fly.

Why can't bicycles stand?
Because they are two tyred.

Why did the biscuit cry?
Because its mum had been a wafer so long.

Why is it difficult to keep a secret at the North Pole?
Because your teeth tend to chatter.

Why don't bananas get lonely?
Because they tend to hang around in bunches.

Why did the clown join an environmental group?
He was concerned about the bozone layer and interested in saving the mirth.

Why did Henry VIII have so many wives?
He liked to chop and change.

Why are aliens green?
They get travel sick.

Why don't cannibals eat clowns?
Because they taste funny.

Why did the apple turnover?
Because it saw the jam roll.

Why does a baker work hard?
Because he kneads the dough.

SHORT AND SHARP

What does BMW stand for?
Break My Windows.

'Ask me, What's the secret of good comedy?'
['What's the secret of good—']
'Timing!'

'Can I see your driver's licence?'
'Not if you're as drunk as I am.'

'You should eat your silverbeet. It'll put colour in your cheeks.'
'Who needs green cheeks?'

Mary had a little lamb, and a side-order of fries.

Mary had a little lamb. The doctor was amazed.

Toby had a little lamb. The case comes up next Friday.

What do *Star Trek* and toilet paper have in common?
They both go round Uranus and wipe out Klingons.

What do you get if you cross a bumble bee and a hypodermic?
A furry with a syringe on top.

Why don't blind people skydive?
Because it scares their dogs stupid.

The man approached the airline counter. 'I'd like a return ticket, please,' he said. 'Where to?' asked the man at the counter. 'Back to here, of course,' said the man.

A little girl goes with her family to her grandmother's. After dinner, the grandmother brings out a cake, which everybody has a piece of. After taking a bite, the little girl turns to her mother and says, 'Well, *I* don't think Nana's cakes are stale.'

What do you call this [hold your elbows straight down against your sides, forearms up and hands out. Wiggle your fingers]?
A shorthand typist.

Should you stir your tea with your left hand or your right?
Neither. You should stir it with a spoon.

Who do you call if you fall off your bike and stub your toe?
A toe truck.

Do you know why the Heaven's Gate people did it?
They wanted to keep up with the Joneses.

Do you want to lose 10 pounds of ugly fat?
Cut your head off.

What did the banana say to the vibrator?
'What are you shaking for? She's going to *eat* me.'

'I'm off.'
'It must be the heat.'

'I didn't come here to be insulted.'
'Where do you usually go?'

Did you hear about the statistician who had his head in an oven and his feet in a bucket of ice?
On average he said he felt fine.

The vampire's wife's had just given birth to a bonny bouncing baby vampire. The attending nurse said, 'Shall I wrap it up?' 'No thanks,' said the vampire, 'I'll eat it here.'

Do you know what the headlines said when the psychic dwarf escaped from jail?
'Small Medium at Large.'

'I'm sharp, I eat razor blades for breakfast.'
'Well, I'm bright, I sleep with the light on.'

Who invented the five-day week?
Robinson Crusoe – he had all his work done by Friday.

There was an elf, a pixie, the Tooth Fairy, the Easter Bunny, Santa Claus, a smart blonde and a $50 note. Who do you think got to it first?
None of them, because none of them exist.

If a person who eats vegies is a vegetarian, what's a cannibal?
A humanitarian.

Why did the girl make friends with the monsters?
Because demons are a girl's best friend.

Have you heard the story about the brick wall?
No? Well, I'd better not let on; you'll never get over it.

First man: 'If I've got $7.77 in one pocket and $32.54 in the other, what have I got?'
Second man: 'Someone else's trousers.'

Two biscuits were walking along a road one bright and sunny day. A big truck came by, swerved to the side of the road and ran one of them over. What did the other one say?
'Crumbs.'

A man in a quiz show was asked to spell *clitoris*. He couldn't, and said, 'This is stupid. I had it on the tip of my tongue this morning.'

How did Rudolph Hess know that he'd landed in Scotland after escaping from Nazi Germany?
He saw the toilet paper hanging out to dry.

A man was in court on a charge of having sex with a horse. 'Was the horse male or female,' asked the judge. 'A female,' said the accused. 'What do you think I am, a sexo?'

A guy goes to see a psychiatrist. He says, 'Doc, I can't seem to make friends. Can you help me, you fat slob?'

This sandwich goes into a bar. The barman says, 'We don't serve sandwiches.'

A bore in a bar was pestering a woman. 'What do you want?' she asked. 'I'd love to get into your pants,' he said. 'Sorry,' she said, 'there's one arsehole in there already.'

There's two types of people. Firstly, there's those that say there are two types of people . . .

My family's into iron and steel. My mother irons and my father steals.

Ours was a quiet wedding; the vicar had laryngitis.

Ha, I fooled the Railways, I bought a return ticket to Wellington and I only went one way.

Have you heard about the girls' brum and dugle corps?

Two guys walk into a bar. The first says to the second, 'Didn't you see it either?'
or

These two guys walk into a bar. 'Ouch!'
or

Two men walk into a bar. You'd think the second one would have ducked.

Sailing a yacht is like standing in a cold shower tearing up $100 bills.

I haven't had sex for so long I don't remember who gets tied up.

Madness is hereditary. You get it from your kids.

A career is what an out-of-control car does when it goes down a hill.

Gladly, the cross-eyed bear.

A dollar saved is a dollar spurned.

I know you're trying, very trying.

Give the police a hand. Beat yourself up.

You don't have an inferiority complex. You really are inferior.

You'd be a fountain without your skin.

You can't walk into the same river once.

Cunnilingus – one slip of the tongue and you're in deep shit.

The only good pole is a deed pole.

November 5. What the Fawkes that?

The end is when the audience walks out.

I'd rather have a bottle in front of me than a frontal lobotomy.

Conserve water – drink wine.

I only go to school to eat my lunch.

I like fortnight tea, but it's probably too weak for you.

Adults are children who've stopped growing up and grow out.

At the end of the rat race you're still a rat.

Seven days without a milkshake makes one weak.

You should be on the stage. There's one leaving in a few minutes.

I used to be conceited, but now I'm absolutely perfect.

I'm on a seafood diet. Whenever I see food I eat it.

The man who walks with his nose in air is very easy to hook.

Keep cool till after school.

There is no life after school.

Take a load off your mind. Sit down.

'Mummy,' said the girl, 'your teeth are like stars.' 'Why's that, dear?' 'Because they come out at night.'

I've told you a million times, don't exaggerate.

'One thing I can't stand about the orchestra,' said the conductor, 'is the random violins.'

It's better to have loved a short girl than to have never loved a tall.

I feel like a million tonight, but one at a time please.

Only users lose drugs.

Yes, I'm under the affluence of incohol, though I'm not as think as you drunk I am.

When I go, I want to go peacefully. Like my grandfather. Not screaming like the passengers in the other car.

If only he'd wash his neck I'd wring it for him.

I hate housework. You make the bed and do the dishes, and six months later you have to do it all again.

It takes a big man to cry, and it takes a bigger man to laugh at that man.

The correct spelling is suck cess.

He who laughs last didn't get the joke.

I had very good karma but one day, oh no, my karma run over my dogma. Oh no. I think I have very bad karma, very bad.

Come with me to the Casbah, and we will have nothing on except the radio.

When the good Lord was giving out brains you probably thought the sign said trains and went the other way.

A liberal is a conservative who hasn't been mugged.

Incest – a game the whole family can play.

I've got three kids – one of each.

All men are cremated equal.

Old soldiers never die. They just smell that way.

Armageddon tired of all this doom and gloom.

I'm confused therefore I am.

Now that you're here, go away and come back some other time.

Did you hear about the two fur seals who walked into a club?

Did you know that smoking is a leading cause of statistics?

He owed his success to his first wife and his second wife to his success.

Nostalgia isn't what it used to be.

Life is a sexually transmitted disease.

You look like a million dollars – all green and wrinkled.

Two peanuts were walking down the street. One was a salted.

Then there was the woman who woke up one morning to find there was a horrible smell – her alarm clock had gone off.

There's three sexes – men, women and teachers.

In a random sample, 63% of American women interviewed said they would never sleep with the President again.

It was so cold in New York that the flasher was showing photos of his donger.

Politicians are like nappies. They should be changed often and for the same reason.

The Indian chief who drank a thousand cups of tea drowned in his own tepee.

Puberty: a hair-raising event.

Lead me not into temptation. I can find my own way.

When a man talks dirty to a woman, it's sexual harassment. When a woman talks dirty to a man, it's $4.50 a minute.

To do is to be – Descartes.
To be is to do – Voltaire.
Doobee doobee do – Mel Torme.

GENRES

Did you hear about the grain that kills people?
It's a cereal killer.

Did you hear they've taken 'gullible' out of the dictionary?

Did you hear that Santa's started being extra kind to his helpers?
He's gotten very elf-conscious.

Did you hear about the two old ladies who went for a tramp?
He survived.

Did you hear about the two acrobats?
They fell head over heels in love.

Why don't Barbie and Ken have any kids?
Because Ken comes in his own box.

Have you heard about the divorced Barbie?
She comes with Ken's accessories.

Why do the Spice Girls sing?
So the blind can hate them too.

Why are there only five Spice Girls?
Because they can't count up to six.

Why did the Spice Girls do a lollipop ad?
Because the Spice Girls suck.

How do you stop a Rottweiler humping your leg?
Give it a blow job.

When's a good time to fake an orgasm?
When a Rottweiler's humping your leg.

What's the difference between a wizard's wand and a bobby's truncheon?
A wizard's wand is for cunning stunts . . .

What's the difference between a politician and a bucket of shit?
The bucket.

What's the difference between Brussels sprouts and snot?
Kids won't eat Brussels sprouts.

What's the difference between the Prince of Wales and a tennis ball?
One is heir to the throne and the other is thrown in the air.

What's the difference between a woman with PMT and a Rottweiler?
Lipstick.

What's the difference between a drunk and an alcoholic?
The drunk doesn't have to go to all those boring meetings.

What do you call a musician without a girlfriend?
Homeless.

What do you call a one-legged virgin?
Hopalong Chastity.

What do you call a Skoda with twin exhausts?
A wheelbarrow.

o ◉ o

What's French, very high and wobbles?
The trifle tower.

A man is in a bank, standing in line behind another man. This other man has sponge cake in one ear and jelly and cream in the other. The man behind him taps him on the shoulder to tell him that the teller's free. 'The teller's free,' he says. The other man turns to him and says, 'You'll have to speak up. I'm a trifle deaf.'

o ◉ o

What has two legs and flies?
A pair of trousers.

What has four legs and flies?
A dead horse.

What has four wheels and flies?
A garbage truck.

o ◉ o

What's brown and steamy and comes out of Cowes?
The Isle of Wight ferry.

What's brown and looks through second-storey bedroom windows?
A shit on stilts.

◉ ● ◉

What's green and goes backward at 150 mph?
Snot.

What's green and goes Doobee, doobee, doo?
Frank Snotra.

What is a marshmallow?
A pregnant aspirin.

What is a Volkswagen?
A pregnant beetle.

What's big, green and brown, and if it fell out of a tree on your head it would kill you?
A pool table.

What's green and goes red at the push of a button?
A frog in a liquidiser.

What is yellow and stupid?
Thick custard.

Have you read *Eighteenth-Century Furniture* by Ann Teak?

Have you read *The Golden Waterfall* by I. P. Freely?

Have you read *The Rusty Bedsprings* by I. P. Nightly?

Have you read *Criminals I Have Known* by Laura Norder?

'Mummy, Mummy, what's a werewolf?'
'Shut up, dear, and comb your face.'

'Mummy, Mummy, what's a vampire?'
'Shut up, dear, and drink your soup before it clots.'

'Mummy, Mummy, I hate Daddy's guts.'
'Shut up, dear, and eat what you're given.'

'Mummy, Mummy, I want to go to the zoo.'
'Don't worry, dear, they'll come and get you when they're ready.'

How many reference librarians does it take to change a light bulb?
'Well, what type of light bulb are you interested in?'

How many Irishmen does it take to change a light bulb?
Two. One to hold it and one to keep drinking until the room starts spinning.

How many men does it take to screw in a light bulb?
One. Men will screw anything.

How many lawyers does it take to screw in a light bulb?
How many can you afford?

How many elephants does it take to change a light bulb?
Don't be stupid, elephants can't change light bulbs.

How many gay men does it take to change a light bulb?
Six. One to change the bulb, two to make the quiche and three to form a chorus and gasp, 'Fabulous.'

How many politically correct gay men does it take to change a light bulb?
That's *not* funny!

How many obsessive-compulsives does it take to change a light bulb?
'If one's gone, they're all going to go. I'd better go and check the others.'

What's the difference between the Warriors and Princess Di?
The Warriors came out of the tunnel.

What did Di have to drink before leaving in the limousine that fateful night?
A Harvey Wallbanger and six chasers.

What did women wear to Di's funeral?
Black bonnets.

Which did Di prefer – a Skoda or a Mercedes?
A Mercedes. She wouldn't be caught dead in a Skoda.

What did Di's chauffeur say to Dodi and the bodyguard?
'Do you want to come with me and Di?'

Why was Di lucky?
She was the first person to see the 1998 Versace collection.

What have Princess Diana and Pink Floyd got in common?
They both had a hit with the wall.

What is the difference between the London Ritz and the Paris Ritz?
At the London Ritz you get after-dinner mints. At the Paris Ritz you get minced after dinner.

What's the difference between Diana and Tiger Woods?
Tiger Woods has a better driver.

Did you hear that Di has something in common with George Burns?
They both died when they hit a hundred.

Did you hear about the princess who stayed out after midnight?
She turned into a pillar of concrete.

Why doesn't Di drive her own Mercedes?
Because she's dead.

When the people at the Ritz asked Princess Di if she wanted a room for the night, she said, 'No, I'm going to crash with my boyfriend.'

Did you know that British doctors could've saved Di?
French doctors didn't have any spare parts for a '61 princess.

Did you hear that the paparazzi were in deep shit in Paris?
Just before the ill-fated Mercedes left the Ritz on that fateful night, they were shouting, 'Di, Di, Di.'

What does Diana stand for?
Died in a Nasty Accident.

Mother Teresa dies and goes to heaven. Saint Peter is there to meet her, and he says, 'Welcome to heaven,' and gives her a small golden halo. Just then Princess Di comes along. She's wearing a superb halo, in fact the biggest silver halo you ever saw. Mother Teresa turns to Saint Peter and says, 'Why's she got a halo so much bigger than mine?' Saint Peter takes Mother Teresa aside and says, 'Things are not always what they seem. It's actually a steering wheel.'

It's just another example of the Franco/German anti-British collaboration that has been going on since 1914. Surely it's no coincidence that the world's best-loved Englishwoman was killed by a drunken Frenchman driving a German tank.

Prince Charles was out early the other day walking the dog. When a passerby said, 'Morning,' Charles answered, 'No, just walking the dog.'

What do Saddam Hussein and Little Miss Muffet have in common?
Curds in their whey.

What do Hiroshima, Nagasaki and Baghdad have in common?
Nothing yet.

A lawyer dies, and, unusually for a lawyer, he goes to heaven. Saint Peter meets him at the Pearly Gates and asks him his name, which he then looks up in his file. 'Okay, gotcha,' says Saint Peter. 'Now, how old are you?' 'Forty-nine,' says the lawyer. 'What?' says Saint Peter, 'only 49?' 'Yes,' says the lawyer. 'But,' says Saint Peter, 'it says here that, on the basis of the hours you've billed, you're at least 165.'

The Pope died and went to heaven. As luck would have it he arrived at the same time as a lawyer. Saint Peter took the Pope with him while he showed the lawyer his accommodation – a suite of luxury rooms complete with a heated indoor swimming pool. The lawyer said 'Thanks' and went into his large private bathroom to freshen up. Saint Peter continued on his way and showed the Pope to his accommodation – a small dingy windowless room in the basement of a rundown tenement. 'What's the story?' asked the Pope. 'I'm the Pope and yet you put me in this miserable room while the lawyer is shown every hospitality.' 'That's right,' said Saint Peter. 'You see, there's a lot of popes in heaven, but we've never had a lawyer before.'

What do you have when you bury six lawyers up to their necks in sand?
Not enough sand.

How do you get a lawyer out of a tree?
Cut the rope.

A gang of robbers broke into a lawyers' club by mistake. The old legal lions gave them the fight of their lives, and they were glad to escape. 'It ain't too bad,' said one crook, 'we got $25 between us.' The boss screamed, 'Bloody lawyers. We had $100 when we broke in.'

After years of hard work, Joe took his first vacation on a luxury cruise ship. Lying back in a deck chair, he recognised an old friend from his home town. 'Hello, Peter,' he said, 'I haven't seen you for years. What are you doing these days?' His old friend looked at him and said, 'I'm practising law. But don't tell Mother if you run into her. She thinks I'm still a pimp.'

This little old lady wants her will drawn up so she goes to a lawyer. He says, 'I'll do it, but it will cost you $100.' The little old lady says, 'I'll be back in a tick,' and goes over the road to the bank, where she asks the teller for $100. The teller gives her a hundred in twenties, and the little old lady says, 'Look, I wonder if I could have a $100 note. I've never had one, you see.' The teller says, 'Umm, unfortunately, I don't seem to have any, but I know that they're printing up a new batch so I'll just go out the back and get one.' So out the back she goes, returning with a freshly printed $100 note. The little old lady pays for this in twenties and then returns to the lawyer's office. She puts the $100 note on the table. The lawyer takes it and they continue with the business of the will.

After the little old lady leaves, the lawyer takes the $100 note out of his pocket and looks at it. He rubs it and, as they come apart, he realises that the old lady's given him three $100 notes – they'd stuck together as they came off the printing press. All that night the lawyer struggled with the ethical dilemma: whether to tell his partner or not.

A doctor vacationing on the Riviera met an old lawyer friend and asked him what he was doing there. The lawyer replied,

'Remember that lousy piece of real estate I bought? Well, it caught fire and I'm here on the insurance proceeds. What are you doing here?' The doctor replied, 'Remember that lousy piece of real estate I had in Mississippi? Well, it flooded and I'm here on the insurance proceeds.' The lawyer looked puzzled. 'How do you start a flood?' he asked.

A doctor at a party got into conversation with a lawyer friend. 'I've got to say that I find difficulty with parties,' said the doctor. 'Someone's always coming up to me to ask me for advice, and I always get caught up in talking to them.' 'I'll tell you what to do,' said the lawyer, 'bill them. Send them an account for advice rendered. That'll make sure they don't do it again with such ease.' 'Thanks,' said the doctor, 'that's great advice.' 'Think nothing of it,' said the lawyer. The doctor went home that night in a much happier frame of mind. Two days later he got a bill from the lawyer.

Steve the engineer dies, and he goes to heaven, and when he gets there he goes up to Saint Peter and Saint Peter's there with his laptop, and Steve the engineer says, 'Hi, I'm Steve the engineer.' And Saint Peter looks through the list on his laptop and he's not there. Not in the big list. So he goes, 'Sorry, pal, you can't come in; you'll have to go down there.' So Steve the engineer goes down there. And Satan's perfectly happy to have him. Now, after a little while Steve the engineer's a little bit dissatisfied so he starts putting his skills to work – and he puts in piping, puts in the aircon, wires the place up. Things are looking good. One day God rings up Satan and says, 'Hey, man, Steve the engineer?' 'Yeah?' says Satan. 'Well, we want him; he's on our list after all.' 'You can't have him,' says Satan, 'he's great – hey, Steve, by the way, put it over there.' God says, 'What's that?' And Satan says, 'Oh, I was just telling him where to put the beer fridge.' God says, 'We've got to have him.' And Satan says, 'Well, you can't, mate.' God says, 'I'll sue.' And Satan says, 'Where is someone like you going to find a lawyer.'

This fellow's wandering along a beach and he comes across a lamp. And he looks at it and he goes, 'Christ, I wouldn't rub a lamp like that,' so he doesn't bother, and he's just about to pass on by when he hears a strangled voice from inside this lamp saying, 'Come on, mate, you know what to do, don't be a dork. Pick me up. Rub it. Rub it.' So he picks it up and he rubs it and, *yah*, a genie comes out. And the genie sits there and says, 'Well, go on, you know what to do.' The guy goes, 'Three wishes, that's right, three wishes . . . Ah, well, first of all, a hundred million in my bank account.' 'Not a problem,' says the genie. *Chuung!* – done. 'Well, I'll have a Porsche.' And the genie says, 'Ah, not a Porsche,' and starts to smile, and the guy says, 'Why are you smiling?' And the genie says, 'Oh, well, it's a private joke really. I was just thinking about the last guy who rubbed me. He was a lawyer, and his last wish was that whoever made a wish after him, lawyers will get whatever it is that was wished for twice. So you've just given every lawyer in the world two Porsches and every lawyer in the world a couple of hundred million bucks.' 'Good God,' the guy says, and then he says, 'I've always wanted to be a kidney donor.'

MEDICAL

'Doctor, doctor, my wife thinks she's a light bulb.'
'Well, why don't you tell her that she's not?'
'What, and eat in the dark?'

'Doctor, doctor, I feel like a bridge.'
'What's come over you?'
'So far, two trucks, six cars and a motorcycle.'

'Doctor, doctor, I don't feel well.'
'No wonder. Look, I'm afraid you've only got three minutes to live.'
'Isn't there something you can do for me?'
'Perhaps I could boil you an egg.'

Doctor, doctor, my hair's falling out. I wonder if you can give me something to keep it in?'
'How about this box.'

'Doctor, doctor, I feel like a pack of cards.'
'I'll deal with you later.'

'Doctor, doctor, I feel like a spoon.'
'Sit still and don't stir.'

'Doctor, doctor, everyone keeps ignoring me.'
'Next please!'

'Doctor, doctor, I can't get to sleep.'
'Sit on the edge of the bed and you'll soon drop off.'

'Doctor, doctor, I think I'm shrinking.'
'Well, you'll just have to be a little patient.'

'Doctor, doctor, can you help me? I keep thinking I'm a door bell.'
'Try these pills, and if they don't work give me a ring.'

'Doctor, doctor, I keep seeing double.'
'Lie down on the couch please.'
'Which one?'

'Doctor, doctor, I think I'm made of liquorice.'
'Well, it takes all sorts.'

'Doctor, doctor, a dog's just bitten my leg.'
'Did you put anything on it?'
'No – he seemed to like it just the way it was.'

'Doctor, doctor, I think I'm losing my memory.'
'When did this first start happening?'
'When did what first start happening?'

'Doctor, doctor, my husband thinks he's a lift.'
'Well, send him up then.'

'Doctor, doctor, my wife thinks she's a lift.'
'Send her up to see me.'
'I can't – she doesn't stop at your floor.'

'Doctor, doctor, I've just swallowed a blowfly. Should I take anything for it?'
'No – let it starve.'

'Doctor, doctor, my husband is a kleptomaniac.'
'Is he taking anything for it?'

'Doctor, doctor, I've broken my arm in several places.'
'Well, don't go to any of them again.'

'Doctor, doctor, I keep seeing Mickey Mouse – what's wrong with me?'
'You're having Disney spells.'

'Doctor, doctor, do you think chocolates are healthy?'
'Well, I've never heard one complain.'

How long should doctors practise medicine?
Until they get it right.

This man goes to the doctor. He's got a banana in one ear and a sandwich up his nose. He says, 'Doctor, doctor, I don't feel well.' And the doctor replies, 'It's no wonder. You're not eating properly.'

A woman was in a coma. She'd been that way for two weeks, since hitting her head in a fall. A nurse came by and washed her privates, and all of a sudden there was a flicker of life. The nurse called the doctor, and the doctor called the woman's husband. 'Did you used to practise oral sex?' asked the doctor. 'Yes, in fact, we did,' said the husband. 'Well, give it a go now,' said the doctor. 'It may be the thing to bring your wife out of her coma.' And as he said this, the nurse pulled the curtain round the bed. As the nurse and doctor left the room, the doctor said to the husband, 'I'll leave you to it, then.'

Hardly a minute had gone by when the doctor heard the husband calling out, and speedily he ran back to his patient. When he got there, the woman had flatlined. The husband was zipping up his fly. 'What happened?' said the doctor. 'Oh,' said the husband, 'I gave it a go, but I think she must have choked.'

A very beautiful girl went to see a doctor. He immediately said, 'Take off all your clothes.' 'Where shall I put them?' asked the girl. 'Over here by mine,' the doctor said.

A chap went to the doctor with severe diarrhoea. The doctor gave him some pills and suggested he keep his bicycle clips on till they worked.

This guy who was feeling poorly went to the doctor. The doctor listened to him describe his symptoms, then got him to piss in a glass beaker. The doctor held the beaker up to the light, mumbled something medical, then dipped his finger in the urine and put it in his mouth. Then he dipped his finger in the urine again and poked it in the patient's mouth. The patient began to dry retch. 'Just as I thought,' said the doctor. 'Weak stomach.'

A young girl went to the doctor for her physical. The doctor put the stethoscope to her chest and said, 'Big breaths.' The girl said, 'Yeth, and I'm not even thirteen yet.'

The patients in a doctor's waiting room were startled when a nun came screaming out of the surgery. She didn't stop to pay her bill, just slammed the door and left. The receptionist dashed in to find out what had happened. The doctor said, 'I examined her and told her she was pregnant.' 'Don't be silly, Doctor,' said the receptionist, 'nuns don't get pregnant.' 'I know that,' said the doctor, 'but it sure as hell cured her hiccups.'

Top 10 things that you don't want to hear during surgery:

1 'Better save that. We'll need it for the autopsy.'
2 'Someone call the janitor. We're going to need a mop.'
3 'Accept this sacrifice, O Great Lord of Darkness.'
4 'Bo! Bo! Come back with that. Bad dog!'
5 'Wait a minute. If this is the spleen, then what's that?'
6 'Oops! Hey, has anyone ever survived 500 ml of this stuff before?'
7 'Sterile, schmerile. The floor's clean, right?'
8 'Okay, now take a picture from this angle. This is truly a freak of nature.'

9 'And now we remove the subject's brain and place it in the body of an ape.'

10 'Could you stop that thing from beating? It's throwing my concentration off.'

RELIGIOUS

The Pope died and went to heaven. Saint Peter met him at the Pearly Gates and took him to his quarters. 'Is there anything you want to do, now you're in heaven?' asked Saint Peter. 'Yes, as a matter of fact there is,' said the Pope. 'There's something I'd like to check up on, about doctrinal history.' 'No problem,' said Saint Peter, 'because here in heaven we have the best libraries and archives in the universe.' So after a couple of days of rest the Pope went to work. Read, read, read. Study, study, study. Finally, 20 years passed, and one day the Pope ran out of the library, yelling, 'We got it wrong. We got it wrong. The word was supposed to be "celebrate".'

The clergyman prayed and prayed that he would see the face of God. And lo! it came to pass.

'I've got good news and I've got bad news,' he said to his congregation the following Sunday. 'The good news is that I've seen God. The bad news is that she's black.'

Moses came down with the tablets from the mountain, and he said to the Israelites, 'I have good news and I have bad news. The good news is that I managed to get it down to 10. The bad news is that adultery's still in.'

God isn't dead; he just doesn't want to get involved.

'Do you believe in sex before marriage?' the recently engaged and soon-to be-married young man asked the minister. 'Not if it delays the ceremony,' was the minister's reply.

Why don't Baptists like fucking?
Because they're afraid it might lead to dancing.

Moses comes to the Red Sea. But how to get across? 'I'm stuck here, God. How'll we ever get across?' 'You're the leader of your people,' says God. 'You'll figure out a way.' 'Oh, come on,' says Moses. 'What do you expect me to do? Part the sea and walk across?' 'If you can do that,' says God, 'I'll see you get a few pages in the Old Testament.'

As part of her final religious training the nun was asked what Eve's first words to Adam were. The nun replied, 'Oh, that's a hard one, isn't it?'

The Pope dies and goes to heaven, arriving there at the same time as a New York taxi driver. Saint Peter greets them both, but is far more effusive towards the taxi driver. The Pope gets a bit annoyed with this, and says to Saint Peter, 'Excuse me, but I'm the Pope.' Saint Peter says, 'And he's a New York taxi driver. He's put the fear of God into a lot more people than you.'

You remember Heaven's Gate, Marshall Applewhite was their leader and they all killed themselves? And they were all wearing Nikes? Well, it wasn't real. It was a publicity stunt. As soon as everybody's used to the idea that they're all dead, there's going to be a TV campaign, and there's going to be this series of ads. You'll see sky, then clouds, then a close-up of the clouds and then like it's heaven and there'll be all these feet poking down through the clouds. And they'll all be wearing Nikes. And the voice'll come on and it'll say, 'Heaven's Gate. Nikes. Shoes to die for.'

The Pope goes to Disneyland and while he's there he's taken on a guided tour. While on this tour he meets the seven dwarfs. They talk for a bit, and then, during a lull in the conversation, Dopey approaches the Pope and asks, 'Are there any three-foot nuns in Disneyland?' 'No,' answers the Pope, 'there are no three-foot nuns in Disneyland.' 'Well,' says Dopey, 'are there any three-foot nuns in Anaheim?' 'No,' says the Pope, 'there are no three-foot nuns in Anaheim.' 'Are there any three-foot nuns in California?' 'No,' answers the Pope, 'there are no three-foot nuns in California.' 'Are there perhaps any three-foot nuns anywhere in America?' 'No,' answers the Pope, 'there are no three-foot nuns in America.' Dopey gives it one last try: 'Are there any three-foot nuns in the *world*?' 'No,' says the Pope. 'There are no three-foot nuns in Disneyland, there are none in Anaheim, nor in California, nor in America. In fact, there are no three-foot nuns anywhere in the world.' At this point the other dwarfs gather around Dopey, and in unison they chant, 'Dopey fucked a penguin. Dopey fucked a penguin.'

A nun returning from a stint of duty in the Pacific Islands learned that her old Mother Superior was in an old folks' home. At the first opportunity she paid her a visit, but the old dear was just about stone deaf. She tried to tell her about the Islands, and started off talking about what she ate there, but had great difficulty explaining the size of fruit. 'The bananas were this long,' she said, holding her hands about 10 inches apart, 'and the oranges were this round,' she said, forming a circle with her hands. 'Father who?' said the old dear.

The ladies' circle of the district church were very upset because an immoral woman had moved into the parish, and rumours started up that she was corrupting the local men. The vicar was visited and in no uncertain terms he was told to approach the vixen and ask her to shift elsewhere. Now the vicar had led a fairly protected life, and this was a very big ask, so he talked a church deacon into going along with him to give him a bit of support. When they reached the gate of the scarlet woman the deacon felt a yellow streak run up his backbone and made the vicar enter the den of iniquity himself. The reverend gentleman was inside the house for over an hour, and when he came out he was smiling, and he said to the deacon, 'What's wrong with the women of this parish? That woman is a pillar of society.' 'Do your fly up,' said the deacon, 'and we'll go back and tell the ladies.'

Two nuns were driving their Mini along a country road outside Belfast when they ran out of petrol. Not far away was a farm, and they were relieved to find that the farmer was of the faith. 'Yes, Sisters, I certainly *have* got some petrol. The only problem is that of finding a receptacle to carry it in. Bottles are at a premium because my sons need them for Molotov cocktails.' He finally decided that the only container available was the big china jerry from under the upstairs' bed. The nuns returned to their car, but it wasn't easy to pour petrol from the po into the Mini. During the struggle a car pulled up and in it was the Reverend Ian Paisley. 'Can I help you, ladies?' he said. 'No, thank you,' the nuns replied, 'we are managing all right,' and they continued to pour the orange liquid into the Mini. 'Well,' said the Reverend, 'I can't say I think much of your religion, but I do admire your faith.'

Patrick and Ikey were returning home from a football do about breakfast time when Patrick said, 'Look, Ikey, if we go back to the flat we will just sleep all day, and I really should go to Mass.' 'That's okay with me,' said Ikey. 'You go and I'll just wait outside.' 'You don't have to do that,' said Patrick. 'You can come in with me. You don't have to take part in the ceremony or anything like that.'

The service had been going for 10 minutes when the plate came round. 'What will I do?' said Ikey. 'Just put 20 cents in the plate,' said Patrick. A little while later the plate came round again, another 20 cents for Ikey, and, lo and behold, if it didn't come round once more!

After the service Patrick introduced Ikey to Father Upper, who enquired as to whether he liked the service. 'Yes,' said Ikey, 'but I am somewhat puzzled.' 'What's your problem, my son?' 'Well, Father, I was taught that the Jewish religion came first.' 'Yes, well, you could be right, but surely that's not a problem.' 'It is, Father, when you think that we gave such a lucrative business away.'

The council in a small town had invested in a new mayoral car. The only problem was, who was going to bless the new vehicle? After a very long council meeting it was decided that the Catholic priest, the Anglican priest and the rabbi would all have a turn consecrating the new car. Before the assembled ratepayers, the Catholic priest sprinkled holy water on the bonnet, the Anglican priest walked around the car six times with a smoking lantern, then the rabbi cut three inches off the exhaust pipe.

Two young boys returned home after visiting a monastery. The first one said, 'Doesn't that wine the monk gives you make you sleepy?' The second one said, 'Yes, and it makes your bum sore too.'

Do you know how to make holy water?
Get some ordinary water and boil the hell out of it.

How do you know God isn't black?
Because if he was he'd go, 'Ah is what ah is.'

The Pope took up golf, and like a lot of people he soon became a fanatic, and quite often called in sick on Sundays. Up in heaven his actions were not going unnoticed, and the Virgin Mary kept God informed of his every movement. One Sunday, after another feeble excuse, he was playing by himself, for he wanted to remain incognito, and he scored a hole in one. The Virgin Mary rushed to God and said, 'What are we going to do to punish him – all this lounging around playing golf!' God said, 'I think he's been punished enough, Mary. Who can he tell?'

One day God appeared to Adam. He wanted to pass on some news. 'I've got good news and bad news,' he said.

Adam said, 'Give me the good news first.'

'I've got a couple of new goodies for you,' said God, 'a couple of new organs. One is called a brain. It will allow you to be intelligent, create new things and hold informative conversations with others. The other organ is a penis. It will allow you to reproduce and populate the planet.'

Adam became very excited and exclaimed, 'With these great gifts what possible bad news could you have?'

God said, 'The bad news is that when I created you I only gave you enough blood to operate one of the organs at a time.'

The Pope was having cardiac problems and decided he needed a heart transplant. On the next Sunday morning after he decided this, when the 40,000 faithful were awaiting his appearance on the balcony in Saint Peter's Square, an emissary appeared in his place. 'His Holiness is in need of a new heart,' he announced, 'so I am going to drop a feather off the balcony and whoever it lands on will be the lucky person who gets to donate their heart to the Pope.' Have you ever heard the noise that 40,000 Italians make when they are trying to blow a feather up in the air?

At the annual fishing contest the wharf was very crowded. Suddenly the cry went up, 'Is there a priest present?' There was no response. Then a chap called out, 'I am an Anglican vicar. Can I be of help?' 'No,' someone called out. 'We want a priest. We need a bottle opener.'

Three priests were returning from a retreat, and it seemed time to bare their souls of their sins. The first priest said he hoped he had been cleansed enough to stop interfering with the children. The second priest said he hoped he had been cleansed of lusting for every new nun he met. The third priest said he hoped he was cleansed of his sins. 'But what are your sins, Brother?' asked the first priest. 'By telling each other our sins in total privacy, knowing that nobody will ever hear our misdemeanours, surely this will cleanse us?' 'My problem,' said the third priest, 'is that I'm a gossip, and I can't wait to get home.'

Three priests were at the bus station, where the girl in the ticket booth had the most magnificent pair of knockers. Because of the great difficulty of keeping their eyes off these monstrous mammaries the priests had to draw lots as to who would buy the tickets. The loser approached the counter. 'Young lady, I would like three tickets to Tittsburgh.' The priest realised what he'd said and he fled in embarrassment. The second priest approached the ticket booth. 'Young lady, I would like three tickets to Pittsburgh, and would you mind if I paid in nipples and dimes?' This priest realised what he'd said too, and fled in embarrassment. So the third priest had to do the job or they wouldn't get to their destination. 'Young lady,' he said, 'I would like three tickets to Pittsburgh, for which I will pay in nickels and dimes. And I must say, if you keep dressing like that when you go to the Pearly Gates, Saint Finger is going to shake his peter at you.'

A short guide to comparative religions:

Taoism	Shit happens.
Confucianism	Confucius say, 'Shit happens.'
Calvinism	Shit happens when you don't work hard enough.
Buddhism	If shit happens, it's not the shit you think it is.
Seventh Day Adventist	No shit on Saturdays.
Zen	What is the sound of shit happening?
Hedonism	There is nothing like a good shit happening.
Hinduism	This shit happened before.

Mormon	This shit is going to happen again.
Islam	If shit happens, it is the will of Allah.
Moonies	Only happy shit really happens.
Stoicism	This shit is good for me.
Protestantism	Let the shit happen to someone else.
Catholicism	Shit happens because you are bad.
Hare Krishna	Shit almighty, hare hare.
Judaism	Why does this shit always happen to us?
Zoroastrianism	Shit happens because someone let the fire go out.
Christian Science	Shit is in your mind.
Agnosticism	Looks like shit, smells like shit, but . . .
Atheism	No shit!
Existentialism	What is shit, anyway?
Rastafarianism	Let's smoke this shit.

GAY

What's the difference between being gay and being black?
If you're black you don't have to tell your mother.

What do you call a gay who works on the boats that cross Cook Strait?
An interisland fairy.

How do you know when you've been burgled by gays?
Your furniture's been rearranged and the interior's been redecorated.

What's the difference between an Air New Zealand steward and a Rolls-Royce?
Not everyone has been in a Rolls-Royce.

Did you hear about the Irish lesbian?
She liked men.

This guy goes into a bar and sits down beside this beautiful woman. 'Hi,' he says to her, 'can I buy you a drink?' 'Look, I'm a lesbian,' she says. And he says, 'Don't you mean a Lebanese?' 'No,' she says, 'I'm a lesbian.' And he says, 'Oh. And what part of Lesbia are you from?'

This guy's in a bar and he's talking to his mate. His mate mentions someone they know and describes her as a lesbian. 'What's a lesbian?' asks the first guy. 'Well,' says his mate,

'see that woman over there? Great looking, eh? Well, a lesbian'd want to get into bed with her.' 'Yeah?' says the first guy, 'well, I must be a lesbian too.'

The little cabin boy goes to his first day on the ship and the bosun's showing him around and they get right down in the bowels of the ship and they're moving in darkened corridors and things and the bosun says, 'Laddie, when we go through the Suez Canal, sometimes the water runs right out of the locks and we have to travel across the land. We usually do it just for a little way and then we drop back down into the water.' And the little cabin boy says, 'But how can we do that? Ships can't travel on land.' And the bosun says, 'This one can. It's got wheels.' And the little cabin boy says, 'This ship hasn't got wheels.' And the bosun says, 'Normally you can't see them because they're hidden because they're under the water. They come into play when the boat goes up on dry land, but you can see them if you look out this porthole here; you can see the wheels if you look down in the water. So have a look out this porthole. Here, I'll give you a hand.' So the little cabin boy looks out the window, leans right out the window, and he says, bent over and looking down, 'I can't see anything. This ship hasn't got any *wheels* [said in a very high-pitched voice].'

Why do sumo wrestlers shave their legs?
Because they don't want to be mistaken for dykes.

You're in the shower with a bunch of guys. How do you find out who the gay ones are?
Bend over and pick up the soap.

These three old school chums get together after years and years and years. They have lunch and then, after a bout of serious reminiscing, they get round to talking about their sons. The first chap says, 'My son's done very well. He's with a top law firm.' The second chap says, 'And my son's done very well too. He's a very busy heart specialist.' At this point he turns to the third chap and says, 'Sorry, old boy, but I heard that your son turned out a bit of a poofter, and I hear he's unemployed.' The third chap answered, 'Well, actually, he's between jobs, but it's all right because he's got these two wealthy lovers who look after him. One's a lawyer with a top firm, and the other is a specialist in ailments of the heart.'

A homosexual arrived in heaven, and Saint Peter told him the rules concerning sexual behaviour. 'You are not allowed to have evil thoughts,' said Saint Peter. 'If you do, your wings will drop off immediately.' Saint Peter handed the man his wings, and as he did so one dropped to the ground. When the man bent down to pick it up, Saint Peter's wings dropped off.

A few days ago the Queen was visiting an old folks' home. As was her way, she'd stop and have a wee chat to the old folks at random. She stopped by one old fellow who was holding some photographs. 'I see,' said Her Majesty, 'that you are into photography. I had a brother-in-law who was a photographer.' 'That's a coincidence,' said the old fellow. 'I had a brother-in-law who was a queen.'

God created Adam and Eve and Adam and Steve.

MALE AND FEMALE

Eight reasons computers must be male:

1 Size does matter.
2 Big power surges knock them out for the night.
3 The lights are often on but no one's home.
4 In order to get their attention you have to turn them on.
5 In case of emergencies it is necessary to have a back up.
6 They look attractive until you bring them home.
7 A better model is always just around the corner.
8 They have a lot of data but still remain clueless.

You have to kiss a lot of frogs before you find a prince.

What do you call a woman with half a brain?
Bob.

What's a woman's arsehole doing when she has an orgasm?
He's usually down at the pub.

A man and a woman are trapped in an elevator. The woman, a virgin, is overcome by the situation and starts taking off her clothes. 'Make me a woman,' she says to the man. The man takes his shirt off, hands it to her and says, 'Here, iron this.'

If it's got testicles and tyres it equals trouble.

What's worse than being a bachelor?
Being a bachelor's son.

What's the definition of a lousy lay?
A guy who fucks you all night with a three-inch dick, then kisses you goodbye in the morning with a 12-inch tongue.

Two guys were walking along the road and they saw a dog licking its balls. 'Wish I could do that,' said one of the guys. 'He'd probably bite you,' said the other.

Do you know why men give their penises nicknames?
Because they can't stand the thought of a total stranger making 95 percent of their decisions.

What is the difference between Government Bonds and men?
Government Bonds mature.

What's a man's idea of helping with the housework?
Lifting his legs so you can vacuum.

What's the difference between a man and ET?
ET phoned home.

Why is psychoanalysis a lot quicker for men than women?
When it's time to go back to his childhood, he's already there.

How do women define a '50-50' relationship?
Men eat, we cook; men dirty, we clean; men wrinkle, we iron.

What's the best way to force a man to do sit-ups?
Put the remote control between his toes.

How do men exercise at the beach?
By sucking in their stomachs every time they see a bikini.

What does a man consider to be a seven-course meal?
A hot dog and a six pack.

Why is it good that there are female astronauts?
Because when the crew gets lost in space, at least the woman will ask for directions.

How many men does it take to change a toilet roll?
Dunno. We've never seen it happen.

A husband and wife have been fighting. It's gone on and on. Finally the husband has had enough. He rounds on his wife and says, 'One more word out of you and I'm leaving.' His wife flings the front door open and yells out, 'Taxi.'

What do men and parking spaces have in common?
All the good ones are taken.

This guy is on a desert island with just a pig and a dog for company. After a while the pig starts looking pretty good to him, but every time he makes an approach the dog grabs at his ankle. It gets extremely frustrating. Anyway, one day he's looking out to sea and sees a yacht capsize. He swims out, and there's only one survivor, who he drags to shore. It turns out to be Cindy Crawford. He gives her mouth-to-mouth and finally she comes round. 'You've saved my life,' she says. 'Is there anything I can do for you?' 'Yes, there is actually,' he says, 'would you mind taking the dog for a walk.'

What's the difference between men and women?
'Wo.'

Five reasons computers must be female:

1 As soon as you make a commitment to one, you find yourself spending half your paycheque on accessories for it.
2 The message 'Bad command or filename' is about as informative as 'If you don't know why I'm mad at you, then I'm certainly not going to tell you.'

3 The native language used to communicate with other computers is incomprehensible to everyone else.
4 Even your smallest mistakes are immediately committed to memory for future reference.
5 No one but their creator understands their internal logic.

What does WIFE stand for?
Washing, Ironing, Food and Entertainment.

Why don't women wear watches?
Because there's a clock on the stove.
Why do women have smaller feet than men?
So they can stand closer to the stove.

Why does it take a woman with PMT four hours to hang out the washing?
It just does – right!

Why haven't women gone to the moon?
Because it's not dirty yet and it doesn't need cleaning.

Why do brides wear white?
So they'll fit in with the other kitchen appliances.

I've been married for a long time. I take my wife everywhere. But she keeps coming home.

How do you stop a woman floating?
Take your finger out.

Why is a woman like a tornado?
Because she makes a tremendous noise when she's coming, and when she goes she takes the house.

How do you batter a woman?
First you lightly flour her . . .

What do you call a woman with a toothpick in her bum?
Olive.

Girls can do anything boys can do. But they're not that stupid.

⊙ ⊙ ⊙

How do a blonde's brain cells die?
Alone.

Where do blondes wash their hair?
In the sink with the other vegetables.

Why do blondes have to have T G I F written on all their shoes?
To remind them that Toes Go in First.

What does a blonde say after sex?
'So, are you guys all in the same team?'

How are blondes and computers the same?
You never really appreciate them until they go down on you.

What's the difference between a blonde and the Panama Canal?
One's a busy ditch . . .

How are turtles and blondes the same?
Once they're on their backs they're screwed.

'No, no,' said the man to the blonde. 'I know what it's called, but it doesn't mean you're supposed to *blow*.'

How do you change a blonde's mind?
Blow in her ear.

There's this dizzy blonde driving along in a red sports car. She's going faster and faster and finally a police car comes up from behind and pulls her over. A policeman gets out and walks up to the blonde's car and asks to see her licence. After a lot of fluffing about, she locates it and shows it to him. Then the policeman asks to see the car registration, which the blonde finds in the glove-box, having forgotten to affix it to the windscreen when she got it. Then the policeman says, 'I'd like you to get out of the car.' The blonde does this and accompanies the policeman slightly off the road, to a spot behind some trees. 'Now, there's something I'd like you to do,' says the policeman, and he starts to undo his fly. 'Not another breathalyser,' says the blonde.

A blonde became so sick of hearing blonde jokes that she dyed her hair dark brown. A few days later she was driving through the countryside and she had to stop to allow a mob of sheep to pass by. While they did, she counted them, then she got out and had a conversation with the farmer. 'I bet I could guess how many sheep in your flock,' she said. 'Go ahead,' said the farmer, 'and if you can, I'll let you have one for yourself.' 'Four hundred and thirty-one,' she said. 'That's right!' said the farmer. 'Take your pick.' Which she did. Then the farmer said, 'If I can guess the true colour of your hair, can I have my dog back?'

How does a blonde switch on the lights after sex?
She opens the car door.

A blonde was sitting in the middle of a cornfield, rowing a boat for all she was worth, when another blonde, driving by, spotted her, pulled her car over to the side of the road, jumped out and screamed to the other one, 'It's blondes like you that give blondes like me a bad name. If I could swim, I'd come out there and kick your arse.'

Why can't blondes get driving licences?
Because when the testing officer says, 'Let's see what you can do in this car,' they jump into the back seat.

A blonde was in a breaststroke race with a brunette and a redhead. They beat her easily. She went to the organisers and complained that they had used their arms.

Two blondes were walking through the bush, when one looked down and said, 'Oh, look. Deer tracks.' The other one said, 'No, they're not, they're deer tracks.' They followed the tracks until they were run over by a train.

There's this blonde and she meets this brunette in a restaurant and they get to talking. '. . . and,' said the blonde, 'I'm not your stereotypical blonde. Why, I know all sorts of things.' 'Well, then, how tall are you?' asked the brunette. The blonde got up, got out a pencil and drew a line against the wall. Then she got out a tape measure and measured it. 'Five foot two,' she answered. 'Okay,' said the brunette, 'how old are you, then?' 'Two tens and a four,' said the blonde, clapping her hands twice and then holding up four fingers, 'twenty-four.' 'Hmm,' said the brunette, 'well, what's your name?' The blonde tapped the table thus: Dum-dum dum dum dum dum, dum-dum dum dum dum dum, dum-dum dum dum dum dum-dum . . . 'Mandy,' she said. The brunette looked at her and said, 'Look, I understand the measuring thing, and I understand the counting thing, but this table-tapping thing?' And the blonde went, 'Happy Birthday to you, Happy Birthday to you, Happy Birthday, dear Mandy . . .'

o ⊙ o

Why are blonde jokes simple?
So men can understand them.

o ⊙ o

A couple had their honeymoon arranged – a trip on a luxury liner. The marriage ceremony went beautifully, and all their friends went down to see the ship depart. It took about an hour for them to find their cabin, familiarise themselves with it and then to unpack. As they unpacked the bride cried, 'Oh, my goodness, I have forgotten my pills. And you'll be playing solitaire on this trip if I don't get some more.' The groom, who had been very quiet, suddenly turned quite pale. 'I'll go and get you some from the ship's doctor,' he said. 'I've got to go anyway. I'm feeling very seasick and need something fairly quickly.' In due course he found the ship's doctor and said to him, 'I want the pill for my wife and something to stop me being sick as well.' The doctor looked at him and said, 'Why do you do it if it makes you sick?'

A man was being pursued by a traffic cop, and he took some catching. 'Get out of the car,' said the traffic cop when the driver had finally stopped. 'You'll need a pretty good excuse for this lot.' 'Well, officer,' said the man, 'my wife left me for a traffic cop, and when you started chasing me, I panicked. I thought you were bringing her back.'

A couple were in bed on the first night of their honeymoon. 'Darling,' said the groom, 'will I be the first man that you've ever slept with?' The bride replied, 'If you fall asleep, you certainly will be.'

Two couples had a dual wedding and went on honeymoon together. After 10 days the blokes were talking, and one said to the other, 'I am getting a bit bored with the same thing four or five times a day. I need a change.' The other bloke thought the same and they decided to approach the girls about a swap. The wives agreed. The next morning the blokes were having a coffee and one said to the other, 'A change is as good as a rest. It was quite marvellous. I wonder if the girls had a good night.'

This chap married a beautiful Spanish senorita, who was extremely hot in the honeymoon bed. All she could say was, 'Make love to me, my darling.' After two hours of non-stop shagging the chap begged for mercy and went downstairs to the hotel bar and had a couple of brandies, and then back up he went to the bedroom for more action. As soon as he got in the door it was, 'Make love to me, my darling.' This bout lasted 10 minutes, and then he begged for relief again. Again he went downstairs. This time he had four brandies, and then very weakly went back up to his wife, but he was finished; he needed sleep. 'What's the trouble?' she said. 'Have you got another woman downstairs?'

A Frenchman was kissing his wife goodbye when she crossed her legs and broke his glasses.

A couple honeymooning in an old country hotel had gone up to their room on arrival and hadn't been seen since. After two days the manager knocked on their door and asked if they were all right. 'Yes, thanks,' came the reply. 'Do you want any food?' 'No, we are living on the fruits of love.' 'Okay,' said the manager, 'but would you stop throwing the skins out the window 'cos they're choking my ducks.'

The general manager of a farm and stock-buying firm picked up a young lady hitchhiker, and as they were going a long distance they settled down to a very comfortable chat. The manager modestly described the size of his business and told the young lady how many people he employed. At lunchtime he bought her a very nice lunch on his expense account and then they continued on their way. The discussion got round to breeding, and the young lady was very interested in this side of things. The manager had to explain in detail how a cow put out a certain odour when she was in heat and then the bull would respond accordingly. When they reached journey's end the lass thanked the manager. Her final words were, 'I hope your cold gets better soon.'

A woman was cleaning the steps when her husband came home unexpectedly. He snuck up behind her and patted her bottom. 'Two pints, please, milkman,' she said.

A man complains to his wife that she never cries out during orgasm. 'How would you know?' she replies. 'You're never there.'

The doctor gave the man the bad news that he only had six hours to live. The man went home and told his wife, who spent the next hour crying. When she had settled, they went to bed and had mad passionate sex. Then they slept for an hour through sheer exhaustion. Then they woke up and did it again. With one hour remaining, the man managed to get it up one more time, and he proceeded to fondle his wife. 'Darling,' he whispered, 'I have less than an hour to live. Let's make love one more time.' 'Come off it,' she said. 'Some of us have to get up in the morning.'

He bought her a drink and said, 'What about a night of sex?' She said, 'Your place or mine?' 'You women,' he said, 'you want to argue about everything.'

NEW ZEALAND

This car pulls up at a dairy in the South Island and the driver gets out and goes inside and approaches the ice-cream counter. 'I'll have 50 vanilla ice creams,' he says to the dairy owner. The dairy owner looks out at the car, which appears to be empty. 'What do you want 50 ice creams for?' he asks. 'One for me, and 49 for the Australians in the back seat,' replies the driver. 'How do you get 49 Australians in the back seat?' asks the dairy owner. 'It's easy,' says the driver, 'once you squeeze the bullshit out of them.'

This lawyer, a tax partner with one of the big Auckland firms, took his wife to the opera for their wedding anniversary. The opera was a bit long-winded and after a while the lawyer nodded off, sleeping till the curtain dropped and the clapping of the audience brought him awake. Startled, he looked around – a sea of blue-rinse ladies, a few elderly gents – and freaked right out. He thought he was at a New Zealand First rally.

How did rabbit calicivirus get into New Zealand?
It was smuggled in in an odometer.

How far should you go on the first date?
Not farther than Putaruru.

Why did thc Maori cross the road?
To make a claim.

Did you hear that Winston Peters was admitted to Tauranga Hospital suffering from self-inflicted love bites?

How do you get Winston Peters to jump into an empty swimming pool?
Put a full-length mirror on the bottom.
How do you get him to do it again?
Put a bottle of Glenfiddich on the mirror.

At Mitre 10, in the timber yard. There's this family sitting round and the father had been deer shooting, and the kids say, 'What's this?' And the mum says, 'Oh, it's something that your father and I call each other occasionally.' 'Yeech, it's arsehole. We're not eating arsehole.'

Sale, a new immigrant to New Zealand from the Pacific, writes home to his mother. He tells her how wonderful it is in New Zealand. 'They give houses away,' he wrote. 'Yesterday I saw a house with a sign that said "For Sale", and today I saw one for my sister Lease.'

A new Asian immigrant arrives in New Zealand, and he's stopped at customs by the customs chap who tells him, 'I'm afraid you'll have to pass a language test before you can enter New Zealand.' The immigrant nods and the customs man says to him, 'Please use the words *green*, *pink* and *yellow* in such a way as to show their meaning.' The immigrant thinks for a minute and says, 'Telephone. *Green*, *green*. *Pink* it up . . . *Yellow*?'

How do you know you're a Westie?
You were conceived in a carwash.

How do you know you're a Westie?
Your mother genuinely admires your girlfriend's tattoos.

How do you know if you're not a Westie?
You've never thought of using lard in bed.

An old woman enters a sex shop in K Road, and in an extremely quavery voice says, 'Do you sell vibrators.'

'Yes,' says the owner, 'we sell vibrators, all different types of vibrators, big vibrators, small vibrators . . .'

'Do you sell the variable speed type?' asks the old woman in her extremely quavery voice.

'Yes,' replies the owner, 'we do.'

'Ah,' says the old woman in her extremely quavery voice, 'then perhaps you can tell me how to turn it off.'

What do Singapore and New Zealand have in common?
They both have more sheep than people.

What's a New Zealander's favourite occupation.
Teloffonist.

What are a New Zealander's girlfriends most commonly called?
*Baa*bera and *Maa*garet.

Did you hear about the New Zealand couple living in a threesome?
The husband was made redundant, and they ran out of money, so they ate the sheep.

Why does an Asian woman buy her chips at The Warehouse?
Because her husband has already bought his at the Casino.

Where do you go if the world's about to end?
New World.

What do you say to an Asian with a driver's licence?
Nothing! [Said while miming fright at having to slam on brakes.]

Three English as a Second Language students were standing in Queen Street on a very gusty day. One said, 'It's windy.' The second one said, 'It's not Wednesday, it's Thursday.' The third one said, 'I'm thirsty too. Let's go get something to drink.'

Morning-tea time at the language school, and there's an ESL pupil who goes into the dining room to make a cup of tea. He takes a tea bag, tears it in half, pours the contents into a cup and adds hot water. 'No, no,' says one of the teachers, who comes in at that moment, 'you don't do that. You leave the tea bag whole and put it in the cup and then add water.' 'Thanks,' says the pupil, and he reaches for a sachet of sugar and puts it in his tea.

A couple of interesting howlers:
The pry minister's office.
The arm defender's squad.

What do you call Maoris on Prozac?
Once were worriers.

A sunny Sunday morning. Two couples were sitting at a table at a café in Ponsonby Road. One of the men, a rather smug fellow, was congratulating himself on how helpful he'd been since his wife had given birth. 'I do my share of waking for the baby in the night,' he proudly stated, 'and I do my share of supermarket shopping and so on. Not that I'm one of these Sensitive New Age Guy types, you understand, not that I'm a SNAG . . .' The other man looked across the table at him and said, 'No, you're more a Caring Understanding Nineties Type.'

I was watching a fight the other night and a rugby game broke out.

New Zealand: the land of the long flat white.

Why didn't the Egyptians and the Maoris go to war?
Because the Egyptians didn't want to leave their mummies and the Maoris didn't want to leave their pas.

What did the truck driver on the motorway say to the tow-truck driver?
Tena koutou katoa.

Two Islanders were walking down the road and they saw their friend Sale stopped at the lights in a spanking new Mercedes. 'Whoa, where'd you get that car?' one of them said. Sale leaned out the window and said, 'It was back there on the road.' 'You mean you stole it?' the other one said. 'No, it's mine. There was a sign on it that said Car for Sale.'

Tukoroirangi Morgan's left Parliament and been offered a job with Dress for Less.

The new Museum of New Zealand logo incorporated the words Te Papa. The logo was designed by Saatchi & Saatchi at a cost of $100,000. Now, one translation of 'Te Papa' is 'the buttocks'. The question is, How much would Saatchis have charged for a penis?

This guy from Wellington goes to Auckland to the Casino. He loses a lot, and when he tries to get a taxi to the airport he finds he's only got five dollars. 'Get out of my cab, you bum,' says the taxi driver, and pushes him out of the cab. The guy ends up walking to the airport. Now, a few weeks later the guy goes up to Auckland again and this time he wins lots. Like lots. He goes to get a taxi to the airport, and he sees the taxi driver from the previous time. His taxi is twentieth in line. The guy goes to the first cab in the line, and he says to the driver, 'How much to the airport?' 'Twenty-five dollars,' comes the answer. 'And how much for a blow job?' asks the guy. 'Get away, you bum,' says the driver, and so the guy goes to the second taxi in the line. He says to the driver of the second cab, 'How much to the airport?' 'Twenty-five dollars.' 'And how much for a blow job?' asks the guy again. And again the driver says, 'Get away, you bum.' And the guy goes to cab after cab. And it's always the same routine: 'How much to the airport?' 'Twenty-five dollars.' 'And how much for a blow job?' 'Get away, you bum.' Finally, the guy comes to the twentieth cab. 'How much to the airport?' he asks. 'Twenty-five dollars,' replies the driver, who, incidentally, doesn't recognise the guy. The guy gets in and the cab pulls away. The guy rolls his window down and as they drive past the line of taxis he goes 'Nah nah nah nah nah' to the other drivers.

Jonah Lomu, Bill Gates, the Dalai Lama and a hippie were passengers in a small plane when it started to go down. The pilot yelled back to these passengers, 'Grab a parachute and jump.' There were, however, only three parachutes. Jonah Lomu took one and put it on and jumped, saying, 'I've got to save myself for the sake of New Zealand sport.' Next, Bill Gates grabbed a parachute, saying, 'I deserve one, because I am at the centre of contemporary technological developments.' And, putting the parachute on, he jumped. The Dalai Lama eyeballed the hippie and said, 'You take the last one, then at least one of us is saved.' 'Not a problem,' said the hippie, 'we'll both go. See, the smartest man in the world just jumped out with my backpack.'

A nun was in a bus travelling between Auckland and Whangarei when it made a stop at Kaiwaka. Two hardly sociable gang members joined the bus. Now, one of the only two vacant seats was beside the nun. One of the gang members sat in the seat and began talking to the nun.

'What gang do you belong to?'

'I am a nun of the Roman Catholic religion and I am married to the Church.'

'What is your arm in plaster for? Been in a fight?'

'No, I broke it when I fell getting out of the bath.'

When the bus reached Waipu the nun got off. The other gang member joined his mate.

'What a rig-out. What gang did she belong to?'

'She said she was married to some bloke called Church.'

'How did he break her arm?'

'She fell getting out of the bath.'

'What's a bath?'

'How would I know. I'm not a nun.'

The Queen was visiting a pig farm when on tour in New Zealand and was shown the prize-winning stock. Among the beasts was a very large barrow.

'What's a barrow?' asked the Queen.

The man showing her around answered, 'That's a boar, ma'am, that's had an operation to stop it breeding.'

Further on there was another barrow, only this one had a ring in its nose.

'What's the ring for?' asked Her Majesty.

'That's to stop it rooting, ma'am.'

'Why, didn't the operation work?'

A man on a plane travelling from Auckland to Wellington decided to make conversation with the young lady seated next to him. 'What do you think of the Australian position?' he said. 'I don't know,' she replied, 'I've never tried it.'

At the end of a micro-surgeons' conference the gentlemen got on the turps and then the stories started. The English surgeon said, 'We had a fellow in a factory who got caught in the machinery and all that was left of him was a little finger. From that I reconstructed a hand, then an arm, then eventually the whole man, and he was so good a worker that he put five men out of work.' 'That's nothing,' said the American surgeon. 'We had a worker trapped in a nuclear reactor and all that remained of him was a single nose hair. I had to reconstruct everything, and he is now so good a worker he's replaced 50 men and his wife is expecting twins.'

'I can top that,' said the Kiwi surgeon. 'One day while walking down the road I caught a fart. I wrapped an arsehole around it and built a body to match. And now it's the Prime Minister and the whole country's out of work.'

A Maori chap in Alaska was on a hunting expedition with three Canadians, and they were snowbound in a little cabin. As you can well imagine, the stories of hunting skills got more and more preposterous. To top them off the Maori told the other three how back in New Zealand they'd catch the bigger beasts by hand, just to be sporting. The Canucks could not believe this and laughingly suggested that he go out and catch a bear while they carried on playing cards. And so, away the Maori went.

A little while later one of the Canucks thought he heard someone calling. They looked out the window, and away in the distance was the Maori running through the snow with an eight-foot-high bear in pursuit. The Canucks prepared their guns. As the Maori got closer they realised he was calling out, 'Open the door! Open the door!' They readied themselves for action, and as soon as he reached the verandah they opened the door. The Maori stepped to one side and the bear went flying into the cabin. The Maori pulled the door shut and called out, 'Skin that one, chaps, and I'll go and get another.'

Two blokes wanted to get into the very lucrative whitebaiting business on the Waikato River near Ake Ake. 'This will be a champion dodge from the taxman,' one of them said to the other. 'He will have no way of knowing just how much we have caught or sold.' They bought a small tin dinghy and some nets and into business they went. The first morning they stood on the bank and surveyed their position, and then, though with no expert knowledge, decided that the far side of the river looked the most promising. Across they went, and after two hours they had two whitebait. They had watched a Maori woman come down to the side they had come over from, however, and after 30 minutes she had a bucket full and went off home. This was too much for our new chums, so next day they stopped on this side of the river and the same thing happened – they got two whitebait in two hours. The Maori woman, meanwhile, had come down and got an old coracle from amongst the reeds, and had gone over to where they were yesterday, and in 20 minutes she had a bucket full. They just had to have some expert advice. So they waited till the Maori woman came back to their side, then they popped the big question. 'How do you know which side to fish?' 'It's my old man,' she said. 'He is the best whitebaiter on the whole of the Waikato. He is also the bloody laziest. When I get out of bed I pull the blanket back and have a look at his old fellow, and if it's lying left, I go left, if it's lying right, I go right.' 'What if it's standing straight up?' asks one of the blokes. 'Bugger the bloody whitebait that day,' the woman said.

A girl was in trouble with the police, and wanted to get out of the country. A seaman said he could help her to stow away on his ship. He and his mates would keep her in food, but she would have to be generous with her favours as they were all risking their jobs. Late at night he took her on board and made her comfortable in a small cabin below the water line. He stayed for a while, to get his reward, then left. An hour later another seaman came in with a coffee and some biscuits. He had his way with her too. Every hour another seaman came in with a drink and food and wanted his share. It came a time when the girl needed a shower, and she asked her next visitor where it was. 'I can't help you,' he said. 'I'm sorry, but they don't have showers on the Devonport ferries.'

A Kiwi in Texas was amazed at the size of the place, and the citizens were not shy telling visitors how big everything in Texas was. The Kiwi went into a huge bar one day and thought, I'll take the Mickey out of these bloody Yanks. He swaggered up to the bar, slammed his fist down and in his best John Wayne voice said, 'Give a man a shot of red eye.' The barman thought, Oh, Jesus, not another one of these clever bastards. He reached under the bar and came up with a small bucket which he promptly filled with whisky. 'There you are, cowboy,' he said, 'a real man's drink.'

'I don't want a drink that big,' said the Kiwi.

'You know everything is big in Texas, don't you, or are you just trying to have us on?'

'No, no,' said the Kiwi, for now there was a bar full of hard-looking Texans giving him the eye. 'No bother, mate, she'll be right. I'll drink it.' He did just that, and his legs turned into marshmallows. 'Where's the toilet?' he asked.

'Go down that passage, about 200 yards and then turn left,' said the barman.

The Kiwi staggered down the passage, turned right and fell in the swimming pool. When he surfaced, he called out, 'Don't flush it! Don't flush it!'

Hori was coming home from the pub one night, well over the limit, and he was stopped at a road block.

'Would you get out of your car, sir?' said the policeman who approached the car.

'I can't. I have a leg injury.'

'Would you blow into this bag, sir?'

'I can't. I'm asthmatic.'

'Well, I will have to ask you to accompany me to the station for a blood test.'

'No, you can't. I'm a haemophiliac.'

'Well, sir, can we take a urine sample?'

'You can't do that either. The government says you're not allowed to take the piss out of Maoris.'

There was an immigration officer who was under scrutiny as no dark person ever got past him into New Zealand. His superiors were sure he was racist, but they had to prove it. A trap was set and he was observed by video and monitored for sound. The first person through that day was a Pom.

'How do you spell cat?' said the immigration officer.

The Pom said, 'C,a,t.'

'Very good, sir. Welcome to our country.'

The next person through was a Dutchman. 'How do you spell dog?' said the immigration officer.

The Dutchman said, 'D,o,g.'

'Very good, sir. Welcome to our country.'

Next through was a woman from the Pacific Islands. 'How do you spell supercalifragilisticexpealidocious?' asked the immigration officer.

A New Zealand soldier returned from peace-keeping duties in Bosnia, and as he had been away 11 months he was surprised to find he was the father of a baby boy just two weeks old. Not wanting to cause too much trouble, he thought he would consult the family doctor first as there just might be a medical explanation. The doctor said it was a grudge baby. 'What the hell's a grudge baby?' asked the soldier. 'It means,' said the doctor, 'that someone's had it in for you while you were away.'

An old veteran had his first trip overseas to Aussie to play in a retired postmasters' golf tournament. You remember when there were post offices? He had minor success and won a cruet set. Back at his own club, where he had a captive audience, this chap – Henry was his name – replayed his big moment stroke by stroke, with the dramatic announcement that there were 5,000 people there to meet him when he landed back at Auckland airport. 'That's a lot of crap,' said a club member, Noel, overhearing him. 'I can prove it,' said Henry. 'You only have to ask the All Blacks. They were on the same plane.'

When God was making the Earth he said to the Archangel Gabriel, 'I am putting life on this planet, and everything will be organised so there is balance. For example, that land *there* will be called North America. It will be mainly white and rich, and as a balance South America will be mainly black and poor. 'What's that white line there, God?' asked Gabriel. 'That's Aotearoa, the land of the long white cloud,' said God. 'That's going to be a special place, full of beauty, lakes, rivers and mountains, and the people will be modest, humorous and intelligent.' 'But,' said Gabriel, 'what about the balance you spoke of?' God said, 'You wait till you see the shits I'm giving them for neighbours.'

What do you call two straight days of rain in Auckland?
A weekend.

What do you call four straight days of rain in Auckland?
Easter.

What do you call two weeks of rain in Auckland?
An Indian summer.

What do you call five minutes of sunshine after two straight days of rain in Auckland?
Monday.

What did the Auckland native say to the Michelin man?
'Nice tan.'

A newcomer to Auckland arrives on a rainy day. She gets up the next day and it's raining. It also rains the day after that, and the day after that. She goes out to lunch and sees a young kid and, out of despair, asks, 'Hey, kid, does it ever stop raining around here?' The kid says, 'How would I know? I'm only six.'

What's the definition of an Auckland optimist?
A guy with a sun-visor on his rain hat.

Meteorological experts predicted a gargantuan flood that would destroy the world. The Pope went on worldwide TV and said, 'This is punishment from God. Prepare to meet your

Maker.' The PM went on national TV and announced, 'Our scientists have done all they can. The end is near.' The mayor of Auckland came on TV and said, 'Due to inclement weather, this year's Hero Parade will be moved to Mission Bay.'

'I can't believe it,' said the tourist to Auckland. 'I've been here an entire week and it's done nothing but rain. When do you have summer here?' 'Well, that's hard to say,' replied the local. 'Last year, it was on a Wednesday.'

What does daylight-saving time mean in Auckland?
An extra hour of rain.

The last person to leave Auckland doesn't need to turn the lights off. They're already off.

How many Mercury Energy executives does it take to change a light bulb?
'We've got four light bulbs. We don't need to change them.'
or

How many Mercury Energy executives does it take to change a light bulb?
'What's a light bulb?'

Of course we have power. My son works for Mercury Energy.

The Mercury Power crisis. It's just not on!

Why did Saddam Hussein hastily sign the UN accord before the Royal New Zealand Air Force Hercules touched down in the Gulf?
Because his military intelligence told him that Mercury Energy directors were on board.

If there's a power crisis in Auckland, what do you turn off first – your cappuccino machine or your air conditioner?
Neither.

Did you hear about the Irishman who got caught in the Auckland blackout?
He was stuck on an escalator for four hours.

Why is the Sky Tower so high?
To give Aucklanders a chance to see if there's light out there.

What did Aucklanders use before candles?
Electricity.

What is Auckland's favourite drink?
Powerade.

How can you tell an Aucklander in a power cut?
You can't tell an Aucklander anything. That's why they have power cuts.

How do you describe a Mercury board member with a torch?
As a light looking for the end of the tunnel.

Due to the present economic uncertainties, and also to save energy, the light at the end of the tunnel has been turned off until further notice.

Once upon a time there were four people named Everybody, Somebody, Nobody and Anybody. When there was an important job to be done, Everybody was sure that Somebody would do it. Anybody could have done it, but Nobody did it. When Nobody did it, Everybody got angry because it was Everybody's job. Everybody thought that Somebody would do it, but Nobody realised that Nobody would do it. So it ended up that Everybody blamed Somebody when Nobody did what Anybody could have done in the first place.

Abandon Shipley!

AUSTRALIA

This Kiwi guy went to Australia, and when he got off the plane and went through customs they asked him if he had a criminal record. 'I didn't think you still needed one,' he said.

There's these three guys in jail in Australia, two white guys and an Aborigine. One of the white guys says, 'I robbed a liquor store, and I got two years, but I'm lucky, it's my first offence, otherwise I'd have got six years.' And he asks the other white guy what he's in for, and the other white guy says, 'Well, I'm in for running someone down in a car. I got four years. But I'm lucky. He might have died, the fella I ran down, and then I'd be in for murder.' Then the first guy asks the Aborigine what he's in for and the Aborigine says, 'Well, I'm in for riding a bike without a light. I got five years, but I'm lucky, it might have been night time.'

Three English girls on graduation from a very high-class school made an arrangement to meet again in five years, to see how life had treated them. When they met and all the greetings were over, the first one said, 'I married a diamond king, and I have everything I want.' The second one said, 'I married an oil king, and I live in the lap of luxury.' The third one said, 'I married a fur king, and I have nothing.' 'But surely,' said one of the others, 'being married to a fur king, you must have plenty.' 'Not when he's a furking Aussie,' came the reply.

Some American tourists were going through the outback of Australia when they came across an Aborigine lying on the road with his ear to the ground. Thinking he had been hurt they stopped to give assistance. 'I'm not hurt,' he said. 'I am listening to a Bedford three-tonner 50 miles north of here with three people in the cab, going at around 50 miles per hour.' 'Good God!' said one of the Yanks, 'you can tell that just by listening to the ground? That's amazing!' 'No, it's not,' said the Aborigine. 'You see, I fell off the bastard about an hour ago.'

The Australian boundary rider was home for a few days and was restless for the outdoor life. He told his wife that he was on his way in the morning. The open range called him. When he sat down to dinner a plate of grass was put in front of him. 'What the hell is this?' he said. His wife answered, 'It's the same food your girlfriends eat.'

A boundary rider was showing a new chum the way of life in the outback. For five days they'd been riding the fence line, and then they came across a sheep with its head caught in the fence. 'I'll show you what we do when we get one as easy as this,' said the boundary rider, and he got off his horse, lowered his trousers and got stuck into the sheep. 'That's the boundary rider way of doing things,' he said. 'Do you want a turn?' With that the new chum got off his horse, lowered his trousers and put his head through the fence.

Australia: as much atmosphere as a fridge, but not as much culture.

What's the difference between yoghurt and Australia?
Yoghurt has a real live culture.

How does an Australian cricket captain count if all 11 players are present?
He opens his fly.

What is the difference between an Australian wedding and an Australian funeral?
There's one less drunk at the funeral.

Scientists have cloned a new breed of Aussie. They're only three feet tall. That's because they've managed to breed the bullshit out.

Why wasn't Jesus born in Australia?
Because Joseph and Mary couldn't stand the strine.

Why wasn't Jesus born in Australia?
Because he had friends in high places.

Why wasn't Jesus born in Australia?
Because Mary didn't want her baby called Dingo Jack.

What do you call an Australian with a chip on both shoulders?
Well-balanced.

A bunch of Ocker tourists were visiting the Auckland Zoo, and when they came to the lion's den there was much laughing and jeering. The sign said, 'Keep well clear. This is a ferocious animal.' The Aussies were in fits of laughter because the lion was lying in the sun licking its arse. 'The poor old bastard,' one of them yelled. 'He can hardly lick his arse he is so old.' Along came a keeper who sternly warned the Aussies to keep away from the bars. 'What a joke,' another one of them said. 'He'd be too old to eat Weet-Bix in milk, and, if he really is the king of the jungle, why's he licking his own arse?' 'Well,' said the keeper, 'he ate an Aussie tourist this morning and he's having a hell of a time getting the taste out of his mouth.'

A sign at the entrance to a lion park at Surfers Paradise gave a warning about alighting from vehicles, and then the schedule of prices. At the bottom it said, 'Poms on bicycles free.'

A Kiwi goes into a shop in Sydney and asks for fish and chips. 'I guess you're a New Zealander,' says the man behind the counter, 'but I have to tell you we don't sell fush and chups.' 'Okay, got it,' says the Kiwi, assuming he's been hassled for his accent. So off he goes, somewhat embarrassed and absolutely fish and chipless . . . Over the next three months he studies the Australian accent until he's got it down pat. Then he returns to the shop. He enters and the same man is behind the counter, 'I'd like some fish and chips,' says the Kiwi. 'Oh, you're that New Zealander, aren't you?' says the man. 'How can you tell?' says the Kiwi, 'I've spent months changing my accent.' 'It's not that,' says the Australian. 'It's just that this isn't a fish and chip shop. We sell clothes.'

There's an American, an Australian and a New Zealander walking down a long dusty winding country road. They turn a corner and come upon a wriggling sheep stuck backside-out with its head between the wires of the fence that lines the road. The American says, 'I wish that was Cindy Crawford.' The Australian says, 'I wish it was Elle Macpherson.' The New Zealander says, 'I wish it was dark.'

A Kiwi couple overspent in Sydney, and they only had $40 left. But they needed money to survive for the four days before they went home. The husband said to his wife, 'The only way to get money is for you to hock your pearly up at the Cross. I'll keep handy so you won't come to any harm.'

The woman hadn't been on the beat very long when a car stopped. 'What's your price?' asked the prospective client. 'A hundred dollars for a short time,' the woman said. 'Sorry,' said the prospective client, 'I only have $60.' 'Wait a minute,' said the woman, and she dashed round the corner to where her old man was waiting. 'He's only got $60,' she said. 'Tell him he can get a blow job for that,' advised her husband.

Back to the prospective client she went. 'For $60 you can have a blow job.' The man agreed and she got in his car and he produced a magnificent beast, firm and ready to tackle any task. 'Do you mind waiting just another minute,' she said, and she dashed around to her husband and said, 'I need to borrow that $40.'

IRISH

An Irishman who'd had a little bit too much to drink fell off a third-floor restaurant balcony and plummeted to the pavement below. A passerby ran to his aid, and asked him, 'Are you all right? Are you all right?' 'As well as can be expected,' said the Irishman. 'Thank God the ground broke my fall.'

What do you call an Irish Rastafarian?
Padlocks.

This man says to an Irishman, 'Have you ever been up a ladder?' And the Irishman says, 'Yes, down a well.'

Have you heard about the Irish kamikaze pilot?
He flew over 300 missions.

How do you break an Irishman's finger?
Hit him on the nose.

Why did the Irishman shut his eyes when he looked in the mirror?
So he could see what he looked like when he was asleep.

What did the Irishman say to the cat?
'Woof woof.'

Did you hear about the Irishman who burnt both his ears? He was doing the ironing and the telephone rang. And almost as soon as he put it down, it rang again.

A beautiful Sunday in spring. The flowers are out and the sun is warm. In the little village church the priest is delivering his sermon. It concerns the Ten Commandments. The priest intones, '. . . and, next, thou shall not commit adultery.' All of a sudden there's a yell from the back of the church, and one Paddy McGee rushes out, shouting, 'Now I remember where I left my bicycle.'

An Irishman goes into a bar. He orders seven whiskies. The barman looks at him in some puzzlement and apprehension. 'Why seven whiskies?' he asks. The Irishman responds, 'Because my doctor told me it was okay to have the odd drink.'

There's an Irishman drinking in a bar. He orders three beers. The barman says, 'You've ordered three beers. Why?' The Irishman says, 'Well, one's for my brother in Canada, one's for my brother in Australia and one's for me. I'm having a drink with my brothers, you see.' Six months later the Irishman goes into the same pub and orders two beers. The barman remembers him and says, 'Only two beers. What happened? Did one of your brothers die?' 'My brothers are okay,' says the Irishman. 'Well, why two beers?' asks the barman. 'Ah,' says the Irishman, 'it's like this. I've quit drinking, you see.'

An Irishman buys a chainsaw. The sales assistant tells him that it's good for cutting down about 40 trees a day. Two days later the Irishman returns to the shop. 'It's no good,' he says, 'I only managed to cut down three trees yesterday.' 'Well, then,' says the sales assistant, 'why don't you try starting a little earlier.' 'Okay,' says the Irishman, and off he goes. A couple of days later the Irishman returns. 'It's still no good,' he says. 'I did what you suggested – I started at first light yesterday, but still I only cut down four trees.' 'Look,' says the sales assistant, 'tomorrow, try working late as well as getting an early start. See how that goes.' So, with this advice the Irishman returns home. But another couple of days and he's back at the shop. 'It's still no good,' he says. 'Yesterday I started at first light and worked till dusk, but I only managed to cut down five trees.' 'Give it here, then,' says the sales assistant, and the Irishman hands him the chainsaw. 'I'll just have a bit of a look at it.' The sales assistant gives the starter a pull and the chainsaw whirrs to whining life. 'What's that noise?' says the Irishman.

An Irish Airlines plane was coming in to land at an airport the pilot hadn't been to before. As the plane approached the pilot said to the co-pilot, 'Look down there, that's got to be the shortest runway I've ever seen.' 'Sure it is,' said the co-pilot. They landed the plane emergency style and finally came to a stop about a foot short of the runway's edge. 'Made it,' said the pilot. 'And that really does have to be the shortest runway in the world.' 'Yeah,' said the co-pilot, 'and the widest.'

An Irishman goes into Pizza Hut and orders a pizza. The man at the counter says, 'How shall I cut it? Four pieces or six?' 'Four,' says the Irishman, 'I couldn't possibly eat six.'

There's this Irish building site, and the Irish foreman asks an Irish labourer to measure the length of a ladder that's leaning up against a newly constructed wall. The foreman says he wants to know if the ladder can be used for working in the as-yet-to-be-constructed attic, or whether it is too long. So the labourer climbs on to the ladder and fixes his measuring tape to the top of the ladder and then starts back to the ground. 'Hold it,' says the foreman. 'I told you to measure the length, not the height.'

Paddy went into a bar where he was well known by all and sundry. He ordered a beer and started on about the races, which horses were running in which race, and what the likely prospects were. The phone rang and the barman answered it. 'It's for you, Paddy,' he said and handed Paddy the phone. Paddy put the phone to his ear, spoke for a moment and shortly commenced weeping, so much so that he could hardly put the phone down. 'What's the matter, Paddy?' asked the barman. 'It's me mither,' said Paddy, 'she's just passed away.' 'Here,' said the barman, 'get this into you', and he gave him a double whisky. Then someone else did the same and so on until Paddy had had quite enough to drink, at which time he left with all the best wishes of the patrons of the bar.

The next day Paddy went into the bar and was very quiet, as a man in mourning should be. After a while the phone went. The barman took the call, said it was for Paddy and handed him the phone. Paddy spoke for a moment, then put the receiver down and started to cry. 'What's the matter, Paddy, more bad news?' asked the barman. 'It's me brother,' said Paddy, 'his mither has died too.'

There was a disaster at the whisky factory when Seamus drowned in the largest vat of whisky in the whole of Ireland. The Inspector of Accidents was called to the scene and set about interviewing witnesses. He asked one eyewitness, 'Did Seamus suffer?' 'Not really,' said the eyewitness, 'although he did skin his knee one time when he slipped going to the toilet.'

A man was spotted one night by the Irish constabulary having his evil way with a pumpkin. The constables stopped and apprehended the fellow, whose excuse was, 'It must have gone midnight.'

As a punishment, an Englishman, an Irishman and a guy from the USA were each sentenced to 10 years' imprisonment, but they were allowed to have one request before they were put in jail. The Englishman asked for 10 years' supply of whisky, the American for 10 years' supply of bourbon and the Irishman asked for 10 years' supply of cigarettes. Ten years later they were let out. The Englishman came out and dropped dead of alcoholic poisoning. The American also dropped dead of the same fate. The Irishman came out and said, 'Anybody got a light?'

When the troubles were at their worst in Northern Ireland, an American radio station decided to do on-the-spot interviews across the Atlantic. The roving reporter was out on the streets of Belfast when he approached a fellow waiting for a bus. 'Excuse me, sir, but I am doing an on-the-spot report on the troubles for the people of New York.'

'What troubles?' said the Irishman.

'But surely, sir, you must have seen signs of discontent?'

'No, nothing.'

'What do you work at, sir?'

'I'm a tailgunner on a milk cart.'

Two Irishmen are walking along. One points to the ground and says, 'Look, a dead seagull.' The other says, 'Where, where?' and looks up into the sky.

What do you call a group of Irishmen standing in a circle?
A firing squad.

The Irish boat people have at last reached Vietnam.

What do you call an Irishman with a small dick?
Justin.

Did you hear about the Irishman who went over a cliff?
He was testing his air brakes.

How can you pick an Irish pirate?
He has a patch over both eyes.

Why did the Irishman stop making iceblocks?
The old lady with the recipe died.

Why do Irish council workers have short breaks?
Any longer and they would have to be retrained.

What is the fastest game in the world?
Pass the parcel as played in a Belfast pub.

Have you heard about the Irish parachute?
It opens on impact.

What is the smallest room in Ireland?
The Irish Hall of Fame.

How do you sink an Irish submarine?
Knock on the hatch.

Why do the Arabs have oil and the Irish potatoes?
The Irish had first choice.

A Yank, an Englishman and an Irishman were drinking in a pub when the Yank said, 'See that man that just came in? That's Red Adair, the famous wildcat oil-well contractor. I think I'll go over and buy him a drink.' When the Yank came back, the Englishman said, 'Are you sure that's Red Adair?' 'Go over and ask him yourself,' said the Yank. The Englishman went over and chatted to Red and bought him a drink. When he came back the Irishman was still a doubting Thomas. 'It doesn't even look like Red Adair,' he said. 'But, whatever, I'll go over and ask him.' He walked over to Red and went directly up to him and said, 'Are you Red Adair?' Red said, 'I most certainly am.' 'Well,' said the Irishman, 'what's it like dancing with Ginger Rogers?'

An oil well in the Middle East caught fire and was burning a million dollars worth of fuel a day. The man most likely to fix this rogue bore was Red Adair, but he was busy in Kuwait, where he had heaps of wells to put out. Someone suggested getting hold of Fred Adair, and offering him a million dollars to put out the fire. They found Fred and his gang holding their weekly conference in the Flying Jug, a famous Dublin watering hole. It took a full five minutes to persuade Fred to undertake the job, though as luck would have it he was actually between jobs. Fred, Fred's truck and his gang were loaded on a Hercules transport and flown to the site in the desert. The ramp was lowered, the truck came down, and went flying straight across the sand and hit the burning rig, knocking it over and putting out the fire. The sheik who owned the well was ever so pleased, and when he gave Fred the million dollars he asked him what he was going to do with the money. 'The foist ting I'm going to do,' said Fred, 'is fix those bloody brakes.'

The Irish traffic cop stopped a car.

'Good morning, Mr Mulrooney. Would you be having your licence upon you?'

'Yes, Officer Murphy, that I would be having.'

'Well, that's good, Mr Mulrooney, for if you didn't I would be wanting to see it.'

The Irish ventriloquist was so bad, his lips were moving when he wasn't talking.

A reporter was interviewing an Irish farmer and was disturbed to see the farmer's dog mount and try to copulate with a cabbage. 'Why is he doing that?' asked the reporter. 'Oh, he's a stupid dog,' said the farmer. 'He thinks it's a collie.'

Some Irish navvies were working on the main city street and when it was time for smoko they wondered what to do. The foreman said to Finnegan, 'Take the thermos into that café yonder and get us some coffee.' Into the café went Finnegan. 'How many cups do you think this thermos holds?' he asked the waitress. The young lady said she thought about six cups. 'Right,' said Finnegan, 'then I'll have three white with sugar and three black without.'

How do you confuse an Irish roadworker?
Give him two shovels and tell him to take his pick.

Seamus was having a terrible altercation outside an hotel, and every time he got up his much bigger adversary would knock him down. 'Have you had enough, Seamus?' asked his opponent as he floored him one more time. 'How would I know?' said Seamus. 'This is my first fight.'

Paddy was in, of all places, Paddy's Market. One stall had a large amount of big pumpkins with a sign saying 'All you can carry away for $5.' 'Well, that's what I call a real bargain,' said Paddy. 'I'll have ten dollars' worth.'

It was O'Toole's first day on the police force, and to break him in they gave him a list of summonses to be delivered all over Dublin. The first few didn't cause much trouble, but then he had to deliver one to the top floor of an apartment building. He left the police car unlocked, and he happened to look over the top-floor balcony just as someone drove away in it. He called in on his mobile, 'Someone has stolen the police car, Sergeant, but don't worry, I got the number.'

A bloke went into an Irish sandwich bar. 'I will have a salad sandwich without any cucumber,' he said. 'I am sorry, sir,' said the man behind the counter, 'but we don't have any cucumber. Would you like it without tomato?'

It was after Mass, and the priest took Sean to one side. 'Look, my son,' he said, 'the parishioners are talking about you and Mary performing sexual acrobatics three nights last week, and everybody seeing you with the lights on and the blinds up.' 'Oh, don't worry yourself, Father,' said Sean. 'It wasn't me. I was on night shift all last week.'

Paddy was coming home from the market with a sack over his shoulder when he met Mike.

Mike said, 'What have you got in the sack, Paddy?'

'Just some cabbages.'

'Let's have a wager, Paddy. If I can guess how many cabbages you have in the sack, will you give me one?'

'Sure, that's a fair bet, Mike. In fact, if you can guess how many cabbages in the sack, you can have them both.'

An Irishman stumbled out of a bar and was apprehended by a policeman. 'Can I help you, sir?' said the policeman.

The Irishman said, 'Somebody has stolen my car.'

'When was the last time you saw it, sir?'

'It was on the end of this key,' said the Irishman, holding his car key up.

'Before I help you, sir, do you realise that your penis is hanging out?'

'Begorrah, they've got my girl as well.'

It was early evening in a New York bar and a chap sat down on a stool and said good evening to the chap sitting beside him.

'Hey, you're Irish, aren't you?' said the first seated. 'I would recognise that accent anywhere.'

'Of course I'm Irish,' said the other.

'Well, saints be praised. So am I. Here, let me buy you a beer.'

They had the beer.

'What part of the old sod are you from?' said the first man.

'Dublin.'

'Really? That's where my family is from. Here, let me buy you another drink . . . And whereabouts in Dublin are you from?'

'We lived in Killarney Street.'

'I can't believe this! Barman, another round of drinks . . . I used to live in Killarney Street too.'

'This is quite amazing. Barman, a drink for everyone in the bar.'

The first man said, 'And what was your mother's name?'

'Her name was Mary, may she rest in peace in the arms of our heavenly father.'

'Well, I'm flabbergasted,' said the other one. 'My mother's name was Mary also, may she rest in peace. Barman, another round.'

Another man enters the bar. 'Hi ya, Joe,' he says to the barman, 'how are things going?'

'Not too bad, Fred,' says the barman. 'Though the grill's on the way out, the wife's a bit sore at me, and, oh yeah, the Murphy twins are plastered again.'

'Hey, Seamus, here's the five dollars I borrowed last week.'

'Thanks, Sean, I'd forgotten all about it.'

'Then why the bloody hell didn't you say so?'

Why do the Irish call their currency punts instead of pounds?
Because it rhymes with bank managers.

An Englishman, a Frenchman and an Irishman were caught with narcotics in a small South American country. They were sentenced to death by firing squad. On the day of the executions the Pom said he would go first as he had a plan, and it would pay for the other two to watch through the grille and see how it worked. His plan was to invoke a natural disaster which would cause the squad to panic. When the commander got to the vital bit of 'Ready, aim', the Englishman called out, 'Earthquake!' The firing squad all dropped their rifles and scarpered, and so did the Pom. Next one up was the Froggie. He waited until the final command, and then he called out, 'Flood!' Again the soldiers scattered, and so did the Frenchman. The commander got his troops back together, lined the Irishman up and went through the drill again, 'Ready, aim . . .' And at that moment the Irishman yelled out, 'Fire!'

Paddy went to the doctor. He wasn't well. The medico gave him a very thorough check-up. 'I can't find anything wrong, Paddy,' he said. 'It must be the drink.' 'All right, Doc,' said Paddy, 'I'll come back when you are sober.'

There was an Irish counterfeiter who was counterfeiting pennies. They caught him because he was putting the heads and the tails on the wrong sides.

The Irish water polo team has withdrawn from all internationals. Their horses have been drowned.

OTHERS

When the black boxer won a world title he became filthy rich, so he bought some land adjacent to the Rothschilds and built a mansion identical to theirs. This did not go down too well with the aristocrats, who wanted to buy him out. The Rothschilds made a very generous offer, which was refused. 'My house is worth more than yours,' said the boxer. 'They are worth exactly the same,' said the Rothschilds. 'Not quite,' said the boxer. 'You have blacks for neighbours whereas I have the Rothschilds.'

A man called Jacob finds himself in dire trouble. His business has gone bust and he's totally in the shit as far as money is concerned. Being so desperate he decides to ask God for help. He goes to the synagogue and begins to pray. 'Please, God, let me win Lotto. I've lost my business, and if I don't get some money I'll lose my house as well.' Saturday night comes and he wins nothing. So Jacob goes back to the synagogue and asks God for help again. 'Please let me win Lotto. I've lost my business and my house and I'm about to lose my car.' Saturday night comes, and still no luck. So back to the synagogue again. 'My God, why have you forgotten me? I've lost my business, my house, my car, and now my wife and family are going to leave me. Why won't you let me win Lotto so that I can get my life back in order?' Suddenly there is a blinding flash of light as the heavens open up, and Jacob is confronted by the voice of God Himself: 'Jacob, please, meet me halfway on this one and buy a ticket.'

There's all these Jews in a concentration camp, and they're being herded towards the gas chambers. One of them all of a sudden calls out to the guards, 'You swine, you murdering Nazi swine!' 'Quieten down,' says the man next to him, 'you'll get us all in trouble.'

How do you tell the groom at a Polish wedding?
He's the guy in the clean singlet.

It's the old days in South Africa, apartheid and all that, and these two security forces guys are hunkered down behind a bit of a dip watching a black man walk along a dusty road. 'Think I'll shoot the bloody kaffir,' says one, 'for the target practice.' 'You can't do that,' says the other one. 'I mean, you've got to have a reason.' 'Well,' says the first guy, 'he's late for curfew.' 'No, no,' says the second guy, 'that's not for quarter of an hour yet.' 'Well, the quarter of an hour will be up by the time that *he* gets home,' says the first one as he raises his gun.

A Scotswoman on her deathbed whispered to her husband, 'I'm so sorry, Jock, but I can't go without telling you the truth. You were nae the father of my children.' 'Do not worry yourself, Annie,' he said, 'for you were nae the mother of mine.'

A Scotsman visiting a house of ill fame enquired if there was any weekly special or if there was a discount on quantity. 'Well,' said the old madam, 'the first is $50, but I will give five dollars off for every succeeding naughty.' The canny Scot got out a pencil and paper. 'That means,' he said, 'that my eighth jump will only cost $15.' 'That's right,' said the madam. The haggis eater went away to a room with a girl and started to give the performance of a lifetime. After eight consecutive naughties he said to the girl that the next one would only cost $10. She started to argue that the score was only six. The madam rushed in to break up the row, and decided the best thing would be for the thrifty one to leave. 'No, no,' he said, ' I don't want to argue. Let's forget the whole thing and I'll start again.'

Young Angus called on the McTavish house one night and asked McTavish if he could take his daughter to the films. 'Aye, I'd let you laddie,' said McTavish, 'but I can see the gleam in your eye.'

The next night Angus returned with the same request, only this time he was wearing dark glasses. 'Aye, I'd let you laddie,' said McTavish, 'but although I cannae see the gleam in your eye, I can see the tilt in your kilt.'

A Scotsman gave a waiter a tip. It ran last.

Why are the Welsh always singing?
Because there are no locks on the dunny doors in Wales.

A ventriloquist visiting the Wild West stopped to talk to an Indian sitting outside a trading post. First he spoke to the Indian's dog. 'Hey, dog, how's it going?'

The Indian said, 'Dog no talk.'

But the dog did seem to talk. He seemed to say, 'I'm doing fine.' The Indian looked shocked.

The ventriloquist said to the dog, 'Does he treat you okay?'

'Yes,' said the dog. 'I don't want for much.'

'Can I talk to your horse?' said the ventriloquist.

'Horse no talk,' said the Indian.

'So,' said the ventriloquist to the horse, 'this is your owner?'

'Yep,' said the horse, 'he is a good owner and treats me well.' The Indian was amazed.

'Do you mind if I talk to your sheep?' said the ventriloquist.

The Indian said, 'Sheep lie.'

The Indians had captured a cowboy. When brought before the chief he was informed that he would be put to death in three days. The chief had a kind heart and said, 'I will give you a wish a day until the end.' On the first day, the cowboy asked to speak to his horse. 'Granted,' said the chief, and the horse was brought to the cowboy. The cowboy threw his arms around his horse and whispered in its ear. Away the horse galloped, returning two hours later with a naked blonde. She jumped off the horse and went into the tepee with the cowboy. 'Typical white man,' said the chief. 'He going to die in two days and can only think of one thing.' The next day exactly the same thing happened, except the horse returned with a redhead. The Indians shook their heads. 'He is going to die at sundown tomorrow,' one of them said, 'and still he only thinks of one thing.' The next day the chief said, 'This is your last wish, white man, make it good.' 'I want to see my horse again,' said the cowboy. When the horse was brought along he grabbed it by the bridle. 'Now read my lips, stupid,' he whispered, grabbing the horse by the ears and twisting. 'I said posse, not pussy.'

An Amish farmer and his family were visiting a mall on their first-ever trip to the city. The father and son were very intrigued by two silver walls in the distance that kept sliding apart and then coming together again, with people walking in and out. Fascinated, they went closer, and stood in front of the lift for some time. 'What is it, Father?' asked the son. 'Son, I have no idea. I've never seen anything like it before.' While they were watching wide-eyed, an old lady came along in a wheelchair and pressed a button, the doors slid open and she rolled into the small room and then the doors shut. Numbers above the door kept going up to 24 and then stopped. Then the numbers started counting down again, then they stopped and the doors opened and out stepped a beautiful woman. The father said, 'Son, go and get your mother.'

It's the '80s, in Manhattan, and there's this yuppie share-broker and he's driving along in his brand-new Porsche and he has this terrible accident. He's so carried away with fantasies to do with his Porsche that he drives into the side of this truck. And he's thrown from the car. He comes to and he sees the Porsche ahead of him, all crumpled up, and he goes, 'Oh, God, my Porsche.' Then he looks across the road and he sees his arm there, which has been ripped off in the accident, and he says, 'Oh, God, my Rolex.'

A New Zealander who had been backpacking through the Far East and the Middle East finally reached Athens. All he wanted was a good hot bath and a clean-up. He booked a cubicle at the Pantheon bath house. He ran his bath and, just as he was easing into it, he had an attack of wind and let rip a reverberant fart. Then he sunk down into the hot soapy water and relaxed. At that moment the door burst open and a Greek man entered. The New Zealander said, 'Gidday, mate.' The Greek said, 'You called me.' The New Zealander said, 'I don't think so . . . What's your name?' The Greek answered, '*Aristotle Plopidopolous*.'

There's this old English gent in the bath and he lets go a tremendous fart. A moment later his butler enters with a tray. 'What's this?' says the old gent. The butler replies, 'I brought what you called out for.' 'What do you mean, what I called out for? . . . What have you got there, anyway?' And the butler answers, '*A hot water bottle and a bottle of olives*.'

Prince Charles shows up at a variety show at a lesser London venue. He's wearing a totally over-the-top Elton Johnish fox hat. The MC meets with him before the show and, when he catches sight of the fox hat, he says, 'Why are you wearing that?' Prince Charles says, 'Because Mummy told me to.' The MC says, 'What do you mean, Mummy told you to?' And Prince Charles says, 'Well, I told Mummy I was going to the Players Theatre, and she said, "Wear the fox hat."'

ANIMALS

Why is a duck when it walks?
Because one of its legs is both the same.
or

What's the difference between a duck?
One of its legs is both the same.

Why can't a duck fly upside-down?
Because it'd quack up.

What goes 'kcauq'?
A duck flying backwards.

Why do ducks walk softly?
Because they can't walk, hardly.

Donald Duck finally got married to Daisy. For their honeymoon they went to stay in a very expensive hotel in Queenstown. There was a lovely view of snow-covered mountains. About nine o'clock the first night they were there Donald went to the front desk and asked if they could tell him where he could get some condoms. 'Ah, sir, condoms, yes . . . in fact, we have some here,' said the manager, handing Donald a packet of Durex. 'Would you like them on your bill?' To which Donald replied, 'What kind of duck do you think I am?'

What mouse walks on two legs?
Mickey Mouse.

What duck walks on two legs?
They all do.

A man went into a bar, put a box on the bar, had a couple of drinks and then asked where the toilet was. Then he asked the barman if he would look after his box of talking ducks while he was gone. The barman thought the man was taking the piss out of him and when the man left he looked in the box. Sure enough, there were three ducks chatting away. The barman said to one duck, 'And what's your name?'

The little duck said, 'My name is Huey, and I've been in and out of puddles all day.'

The barman said to another duck, 'What's your name, and what have you been doing today?'

'My name is Dewey, and I have been in and out of puddles all day.'

The barman then turned to the third duck and said, 'I suppose your name is Louie?'

'Oh, no,' said the duck, 'my name is Puddles and I've had a prick of a day.'

'What's your cat called?'
'Ben Hur.'
'Why did you call it that?'
'Well, we called it Ben, but then we found out it was a girl.'

Once upon a time there was a sparrow who decided not to fly south for the winter. For a while things were fine, but then he started to get really cold, and he finally decided that he'd better join his friends on the southward migration. So he took off, and flew high above the farmyard, but it was so cold that his wings froze and he plummeted to the ground.

Just then a cow came by and shat on the sparrow. 'Oh, ah, gross,' he thought. But then when he realised that the warmth of the cowshit had thawed out his wings he was jubilant and shook his wings and burst loudly into song.

A cat, sleeping beneath the barn, woke when he heard the sparrow, and crept up on him and pulled him out of the pile of shit and ate him.

The moral of the story is:

1 Not everyone who shits on you is your enemy.
2 Not everyone who gets you out of the shit is your friend.
3 If you're warm and happy in your pile of shit, for God's sake keep your mouth shut.

What do you get if you cross a kangaroo with a lamb?
A little woolly jumper.

There are three polar bears sitting on an icefloe in the Arctic, a mummy polar bear, a daddy polar bear and a little weeny baby polar bear. The little baby polar bear says to his mother, 'Mummy, Mummy, are you sure I'm a polar bear?'

'Yes, dear,' says his mother, 'of course you're a polar bear.'

Then the little baby polar bear turns to his father and says, 'Daddy, Daddy, are you sure I'm a polar bear?'

And his father says, 'Yes, son, of course you're a polar bear.'

'Are you absolutely sure?' says the little baby polar bear. 'You're sure I'm not perhaps some other kind of bear?'

'No, son,' says his father. 'I'm a polar bear and your mother is a polar bear and, therefore, you are a polar bear . . . Why do you ask?'

'Because I'm absolutely freezing,' says the little baby polar bear.

Where do lizards go to relax?
The lounge.

A man goes into a bar with a giraffe. He orders a drink for himself and one for the giraffe as well. After a while he orders another drink for himself and another drink for the giraffe. This goes on for quite a while. Finally, the giraffe is so drunk he collapses on the floor where he goes soundly to sleep. The man gets up and starts for the door. 'Hey,' the barman calls after him, 'you're not going to leave that lying there, are you?' 'It's not a lion,' answers the man, 'it's a giraffe.'

Did you know that the equator is a non-existent animal?
It's an imaginary lion that runs around the middle of the Earth.

A hunter is walking through the jungle and he comes to a clearing where he sees a dead lion. Looking closely, he sees that there's a mouse sitting on the lion. 'What happened here, then?' asks the hunter. 'What happened,' says the mouse, 'is that I killed this lion.' At this the hunter looks surprised. 'Well, to be precise,' says the mouse, 'I killed it with my club.' 'That's absolutely amazing,' says the hunter. 'Yes,' says the mouse, 'there's about 30 of us, actually.'

What do you call eight cats?
Octopus.

What did the boy octopus say to the girl octopus?
I want to hold your hand hand hand hand hand hand hand hand . . .

A guy was touring the world with an octopus which could play most any instrument you could name. He was making a lot of gold because the octopus was very talented. In a bar one night the octopus had entertained a large crowd on many types of instruments. A fellow held up a set of bagpipes and said, 'What can you do with these?' The octopus, who'd never actually seen bagpipes before and they were therefore one of the few instruments he couldn't play, studied the bagpipes intently. The owner said to the man, 'Show him how. Go on, hurry up and play something on the damn thing.' 'Yes, play it,' said the octopus, 'otherwise I'll rip its pyjamas off and fuck it.'

What did the bull say to the cow?
'When I fall in love it will be for heifer.'

Have you heard the one about the bulls in the paddock?
We'd better not tell you – it's full of bullshit.

There's two cows standing in a field. One says, 'Moo.' The other says, 'I was going to say that.'

An old bull and a young bull were standing in a paddock looking at the cows in the next paddock when they noticed that the gate between the paddocks had been left open. 'Look at that,' said the young bull. 'Let's dash down there and hump a couple.' 'No,' said the old bull, 'let's stroll down there very casually and hump the lot.'

What do you get when you cross a pig and a centipede?
Bacon and legs.

What is a myth?
A female moth.

What's got four legs and one arm?
A happy pit bull terrier.

Two farmers were arguing as to who had the cleverest dog. The first farmer said, 'I can give my dog 10 commands and he will carry them out in the exact order.' This he did and the dog performed perfectly. The second farmer said, 'I can give my dog 12 commands and he will carry them out in the exact order. Plus, my dog can read.' His dog was down by the gate, and he called it and he called it but it would not move. Fearing that the dog might be injured the two farmers went down to the gate to find the dog with his paw on a $20 bill.

How did the fleas get from Auckland to Wellington?
They itch-hiked.

Two green caterpillars were munch, munch, munching away at a swan plant. A Monarch butterfly flew past.

'Gosh!' said one of the caterpillars, *munch, munch, munch*, 'I wouldn't be seen dead in one of those things.'

Why did the koala fall out of the tree?
Because it was dead.
Why did the second koala fall out of the tree?
Because it got hit by the first koala.
Why did the third koala fall out of the tree?
Because it thought it was a game.

What do birds have for breakfast?
Tweetbix.

What's the best way to catch a fish?
Get someone to throw one at you.

What do you call a bunch of rabbits walking backwards?
A receding hare line.

What's the best way to hunt bear?
With your clothes off.

What do you have to know before teaching tricks to your dog?
More than the dog.

The postman looked at the formidable dog lying on the front doorstep. He said to the lady of the house, 'What kind of dog is that?'

'I don't rightly know. My brother sent it to me from Africa.'

'Well,' said the postman, 'it's the oddest dog that I've ever seen.'

The woman nodded her head and said, 'You should have seen it before I cut its mane off.'

How do you stop your dog barking in the back seat of your car?
Put him in the front seat.

What do you call a cow with no legs?
A ranchslider.

What do you call a cow with no legs?
Ground beef.

What do you call a cow with three legs?
Lean beef.

What do you call a sheep with no legs?
A cloud.

What do you call an antelope with good vision?
A good idea.
What do you call a bird with good vision?
A seagull.

How does a sparrow exit a plane?
With a sparrowshute.

What do you call a gorilla with a machine-gun?
Sir.

What do you give a gorilla with a machine-gun ?
Anything he wants!

A gorilla walks into a bar, pulls up a stool and orders a beer. The barman serves him and asks for five dollars, and adds, 'You know, we don't get many gorillas in here.' To which the gorilla replies, 'At five bucks a beer, it's no wonder.'

Where do you find a turtle with no legs?
Where you left it.

Why do bees hum?
Because they don't know the words.

What's the difference between a buffalo and a bison?
You can't wash your hands in a buffalo.

What do you call a blind dinosaur?
A Doyouthinkhesawus.

What do you call a blind dinosaur's dog?
A Doyouthinkhesawus Rex.

A salesman selling insurance was calling on farms, and as he approached this particular farmhouse he noticed a pig with a wooden leg hobbling about. He knocked on the door and introduced himself and showed his credentials. 'Before I tell you what my company has to offer, I just have to know about the pig with the wooden leg,' he said. 'Oh,' said the lady of the house, 'that's Mr Piggy. He's amazing. One night the house caught fire and he made such a fuss that he woke us up, and thus he saved our lives. On another occasion the bridge was down during a flood and I ran into the river in the car. I had the kids with me. Mr Piggy saw what happened from a nearby field, and he ran home and got my husband, who pulled us out with a tractor. So he saved our lives a second time.' 'But what about the wooden leg?' said the salesman. The woman answered, 'Well, if you had a pig that valuable you wouldn't eat him all at once, would you?'

A chicken farmer acquired a rooster. The rooster came highly recommended, but was also very expensive. The farmer put the rooster in the fowl run with the intention of later on eating the old rooster for dinner. The new cock strutted around the fowl yard stopping only to preen his magnificent feathers. Then the time came for the fight, for he had to beat the hell out of the old rooster, as it was the law of the yard. Now, the old fellow had been around for a long time and was also a great negotiator, and it was in this spirit that he approached the new bird. 'I say there, young fellow, I know it's about time we had the big fight, but it's a stupid custom. You will win, but as you can see I am still in pretty good nick and I have no doubt that I will do considerable damage to you. Now, I have a plan. We could have a race around the yard. You give me a bit of a start; a couple of laps ought to be enough to impress the ladies; and he who wins the race runs the yard.' The young rooster thought this was a great idea. To give atmosphere to the proceedings the old fellow asked all the hens to cheer and flap their wings, and the big race started. The farmer, hearing all the squawking, thought a fox might have got into the run, so he grabbed his gun, and he'd just got to the yard as the young rooster caught up with the old one. The farmer didn't hesitate – up with the gun and he shot the young bird. 'All that money,' he muttered, 'and I get a queer one.'

When the little frog went missing her mother found her sitting on a toadstool.

A new chum in the Antarctic found the enforced celibacy was getting to him, so he approached the chief with his worries. The chief gave him the bad news first, that there wouldn't be any more planes in until the winter had ended. The good news was that the yak down in the stables was known to be friendly, especially if you went down armed with some sugar. The bloke went down, but forgot the sugar. He had his wicked way, and then the yak said, 'Where's my sugar?' The bloke ignored the animal. 'That's typical,' said the yak. 'Fuck you, Yak, I'm all right.'

A guy went to a pet shop to buy a parrot. He wanted a good talker. 'Which is the best talker in your collection?' he asked the pet shop owner. The proprietor took him over to a vividly coloured macaw. 'This bird is brilliant,' he said, 'but I must warn you he has a very foul mouth. He never shuts up, and can be extremely filthy.' 'If he can talk that well,' said the guy, 'then he must be an intelligent bird and I'm sure I'll be able to train him to clean up his speech.' He took the bird home and it never shut up. It let out one long stream of profanities after another. The guy gave the bird several warnings, and in exasperation he finally shoved it in the freezer to cool down. After a few minutes he let it out and it jumped up on to his shoulder. 'Okay, I'll tone down and behave,' it said. Then the parrot said, 'And, by the way, what did the chicken do?'

A grasshopper walks into a bar, pulls up a stool and orders a beer. The barman pours the beer and says, 'Do you know we have a drink named after you?' To which the grasshopper replies, 'You have a drink called Bob?'

ELEPHANTS

Why did the elephant paint the soles of his feet yellow?
So he could hide upside-down in a bowl of custard.
Have you ever seen an elephant hiding upside-down in a bowl of custard?
[No.] Well, that just shows how effective it is.

What do you get if you cross a kangaroo with an elephant?
Great big holes all over Africa.

Why are elephants wrinkled?
Have you ever tried ironing one?

Why did the elephants have to get out of the swimming pool?
Because they couldn't keep their trunks up.

How do you get an elephant into a matchbox?
First, you take out all the matches.

Why did the elephant wear springs on his feet?
So he could jump up and catch the monkeys.
What is the most feared noise in the jungle?
Boing boing boing.

Can an elephant jump higher than a lamp post?
Yes. Lamp posts can't jump.

What's big, grey and mutters?
A mumbo jumbo.

How do you raise a baby elephant that's been abandoned by its parents?
With a fork-hoist.

What's big and sings?
Elephantsgerald.

How do you stop an elephant charging?
Take away his credit cards.

Why are elephants big, grey and wrinkly?
Because if they were small, white and round they'd be aspirins.

How can you tell if there's an elephant in your bed?
There is an E on his pyjamas.

How can you tell when there's an elephant under the bed?
When you're nearly touching the ceiling.

What goes out grey and comes back white?
An elephant that's been in a snow storm.

What do you give to a nervous elephant?
Trunkquillisers.

What did the river say when the elephant sat in it?
'Well, I'll be damned.'

How does an elephant get to the top of an oak tree?
It sits on an acorn and waits for it to grow.

How does an elephant get down from an oak tree?
It sits on a leaf and waits for autumn.

What is grey and comes in quarts?
An elephant.

What would you get if you crossed an elephant and a rug?
A deep pile carpet.

How do you get down off an elephant?
You don't get down off an elephant, silly, you get it off a duck.

What time is it when an elephant sits on your fence?
Time to get a new one.

What do you call an elephant wearing pink earmuffs and a dress?
Anything you want, it can't hear you.

Why do elephants drink so much?
To try to forget.

What's grey, yellow, grey, yellow, grey, yellow, grey, yellow, grey, yellow, grey, yellow?
An elephant rolling down a hill with a daisy in its mouth.

Why did the elephant stand on the marshmallow?
So she wouldn't fall in the hot chocolate.

What's grey and white on the inside and red on the outside?
An inside-out elephant.

What's grey and white on the inside and red and white on the outside?
Campbell's Cream of Elephant Soup.

How does an elephant hide in the jungle?
He paints his balls red and sits in a cherry tree.
What's the loudest noise in the jungle?
A native eating cherries.

What's the biggest drawback of the jungle?
An elephant's foreskin.

How many legs does an elephant have?
Four. Two at the front, two at the back.

What was the elephant doing on the motorway?
About eight kilometres per hour.

How do you know if you pass an elephant?
You can't get the toilet seat down.

How do you get an elephant into a VW bug?
Open the car door, put the elephant inside and close the door.

What's more difficult than getting a pregnant elephant in a VW bug?
Getting an elephant pregnant in a VW bug.

How do you put an elephant into a fridge?
Open the VW door, take the elephant out, close the VW door, open the fridge, put the elephant inside, close the fridge.

How do you know if there's an elephant in your fridge?
Footprints in the butter.

How do you know if there are two elephants in your fridge?
Two sets of footprints in the butter.

How do you know if there are three elephants in your fridge?
You can't get the fridge door closed.

How do you know if there are four elephants in your fridge?
There's a VW bug parked outside it.

How do you get eight elephants in your fridge?
Put four in a VW, four in another VW and then put the two VWs in the fridge. A fridge large enough to hold two elephants can surely hold two VWs.

How do you get Tarzan in the fridge?
Open the door, get the two VWs out, put Tarzan in, close the door.

How do you know Tarzan is in the fridge?
You can hear him scream, OYOYOYOIYOIYOOOOOO!

How do you get two Tarzans in the fridge?
You can't, silly. There is only one Tarzan.

Why are there so many elephants running around free in the jungle?
The fridge isn't large enough to hold them all.

How many elephants can you actually put in a fridge?
Depends on the number of elephants.

What did the fifth elephant in the VW bug discover?
The sun roof.

The lion (the king of the animals) gathered all the animals for a meeting. All of them showed up except the elephants. Why?
They were stuck in the VW bug.

How many giraffes can you fit in a VW bug?
None, it's full of elephants.

What do you call two elephants on a bicycle?
Optimistic.

What do you get if you take an elephant into the city?
Free parking.

What do you get if you take an elephant into work?
Sole use of the elevator.

How do you know if there is an elephant in the pub?
Its bike is outside.
How do you know if there are two elephants in the pub?
There is a dent in the cross-bar.
How do you know if there are three elephants in the pub?
You stand on the bike and have a look in the window.

Why do elephants wear tiny green hats?
So they can sneak across a pool table without being seen.

What do you get if you cross an elephant with a whale?
A submarine with a built-in snorkel.

Why do elephants wear sandals?
So that they don't sink in the sand.
Why do ostriches stick their heads in the ground?
To look for the elephants who forgot to wear their sandals.

What is the difference between an elephant and a blueberry?
They're both blue, except for the elephant.

How do you make a dead elephant float?
Well, you take 10 dead elephants, 10 tonnes of chocolate ice cream, five tonnes of bananas . . .

Why do ducks have flat feet?
From stamping out forest fires.
Why do elephants have flat feet?
From stamping out flaming ducks.

Why shouldn't you go into the woods at five o'clock?
Because that is when the elephants practice their parachute jumping.
What is a furry alligator?
A bear that went into the woods at five o'clock.
Why are pygmies so short?
They can't tell time.
What is that stuff between elephants' toes?
Watchless natives.

What do you know when you see three elephants walking down the street wearing pink sweatshirts?
That they're all on the same team.

What is an elephant's sex organ?
His foot. If he steps on you, you're fucked.

What do you call an elephant who is an expert on skin disorders?
A pachydermatologist.

What do you get when you cross an elephant with a hooker?
A two-tonne pickup.

What did the female elephant say after sex?
'Can I be on top next time?'

Why do elephants have trunks?
Because they would look silly with glove compartments.

What do you do when you come across an elephant?
Wipe it off.

Have you heard about Hannibal crossing the Alps with elephants?
None of the offspring survived.

How does the male elephant find the female elephant when she's lying down in tall grass?
Very attractive.

What did the elephant say when he saw a dead ant on the road?
Deadant, deadant, deadant deadant [to be sung].
What did the elephant say when he saw a live ant on the road?
He stamped it to death and then said, 'Deadant, deadant, deadant deadant.'

What do you give a seasick elephant?
Lots of room.

What do you do if an elephant comes through your window?
Swim for your life.

Why do elephants lay on their backs?
To trip low-flying canaries.

Why do elephants have big ears?
Because Noddy won't pay the ransom.

How can you tell when elephants have been making love in your back yard?
The fence is broken and one of your rubbish bags is gone.

How do you make an elephant fly?
Start with a three-foot zipper.

What has two tails, two trunks and five feet?
An elephant with spare parts

What is the height of ambition?
An ant climbing an elephant's leg with the intention of rape.

What's grey and puts out forest fires?
Smokey the Elephant.

What happens when an elephant sits in front of you at the movies?
You miss most of the picture.

What do elephants use for slippers?
Sheep.

Getting anything done around here is like mating elephants:
1 It's done on a very high level.
2 There's a lot of stomping and screaming involved.
3 It takes two years to get any results.

It says in a book that more than 6000 elephants go each year to make piano keys. Isn't it amazing what elephants can be trained to do?

Every nation has to write a book about the elephant:
The French book – *The Sex Life of the Elephant*; or, *1000 Ways to Cook Elephant*
The English book – *Elephants I Have Shot on Safari*
The Welsh book – *The Elephant and Its Influence on Welsh*

Language and Culture; or, *Oes ysgol tocynnau eleffant llanfairpwll nhadau coeden*
The American book – *How To Make Bigger and Better Elephants*
The Japanese book – *How To Make Smaller and Cheaper Elephants*
The Greek book – *How To Sell Elephants for a Lot of Money*
The Finnish book – *What Do Elephants Think about Finnish People?*
The German book – *A Short Introduction to Elephants, Vols 1-6*
The Icelandic book – *Defrosting an Elephant*
The Swiss book – *Switzerland: The Country through Which Hannibal Went with His Elephants*
The Canadian book – *Elephants: A Federal or a State Issue?*
The Swedish book – *How To Reduce Your Taxes with an Elephant.*

Hickory Dickory Dock,
An elephant ran up the clock . . .
The clock is currently being repaired.

A foolproof method for sculpting an elephant: first, get a huge block of marble; then you chip away everything that doesn't look like an elephant.

An ant and an elephant share a night of romance. Next morning the ant wakes up and the elephant is dead. 'Damn,' says the ant, 'one night of passion and I spend the rest of my life digging a grave.'

A mouse found an elephant suffering with a thorn in its foot, and he duly obliged by removing the offending thorn. The elephant was so thankful that she told the mouse he could have anything he wanted. 'Well,' said the mouse, 'I'm a randy little so-and-so and it would be something if I could tell the boys that I'd shagged an elephant.' The elephant agreed and backed against a tree so the mouse could climb up. The mouse climbed up and jumped on to the elephant, and thus began a most unusual sexual encounter. Just then a native hunting party saw enough food for the whole tribe and they threw their spears, catching the elephant behind the ears, making the animal lurch violently. The mouse called out, 'I didn't hurt you, did I?'

It was a boring Sunday afternoon in the jungle, so the elephants decided to challenge the ants to a game of soccer. The game was going well, with the elephants beating the ants 10 goals to nil, when the ants gained possession.

The ants' star player was dribbling the ball towards the elephants' goal when the elephants' left back came lumbering towards him. The elephant trod on the little ant, killing him instantly.

The referee stopped the game. 'What the hell do you think you're doing? Do you call that sportsmanship, killing another player?'

The elephant replied, 'Well, I didn't mean to kill him – I was just trying to trip him up.'

There was this guy who bought an elderly circus elephant. I don't know why. Alas, though, he couldn't afford to feed it. Now, he'd never seen an elephant jump with all four feet off the ground, so he started a contest: entry was $10, and the first person to get the elephant to jump with all four feet off the ground would get $50,000.

All sorts of people tried, but nobody could get the elephant to jump. Finally, this little guy arrives in a limousine. He's carrying a baseball bat. He walks up to the elephant, swings the bat and crunches the elephant's balls pretty badly. Needless to say, the elephant jumps, and the owner pays out the $50,000.

Unfortunately, the owner had barely collected enough to cover the prize, so he ran another contest. He'd never seen an elephant shake its head back and forth as if to say No, so he thought he'd give that a go. Same deal as before: $10 per entry, $50,000 prize. Lots of people tried and failed. Then the little guy shows up in his limousine again, pulls out his bat and walks up to the elephant. He says, 'Remember me?' The elephant nods Yes. The man holds up his bat and says, 'Want me to use this again?' The elephant shakes his head rather emphatically No.

One afternoon, there was this good witch who was flying along when, all of a sudden, she heard this soft crying from down below. When she landed, she saw this yellow frog. Touched by his sadness, the witch asked why he was crying. 'Sniff. None of the other frogs will let me join in their frog games. Boo hoo.'

'Don't cry, little one,' replied the witch and, with a wave of her magic wand, the frog turned green. All happy now, the frog was checking himself over when he noticed that his penis was still yellow. He asked an embarrassed witch about this, and she told him that there were some things that she just couldn't do, but, if he saw the wizard, he'd fix things up for him. So happily, the little green frog hippity-hopped along his merry way.

Feeling quite happy about herself, the witch once more took to the skies and, once again, she heard some crying, but this time of a thunderous sort. So down to the ground she flew, only to discover a pink elephant. The witch asked him why he was crying. 'Sniff. None of the other elephants will let me join in their elephant games. Boo hoo.'

Now if you have ever seen an elephant cry, you know it to be a pathetic-looking sight, but a pink elephant crying is just downright heart-breaking, and that is just how the witch felt, as if her heart were breaking. So, once again, she waved her magic wand, and *poof*, the elephant was grey.

All happy now, the elephant was checking himself over when he noticed that his penis was still pink. He asked an embarrassed witch about this, and she told him that there were some things that she just couldn't do, but, if he saw the wizard, he would fix things up for him.

At this point, the elephant just started wailing. 'I don't know where the wizard is,' he sobbed.

'Oh, that's easy,' said the witch, 'just follow the yellow pricked toad.'

AGE

A 92-year-old man is having an affair with an incredibly beautiful 20-year-old blonde. One day he goes to confession and he tells the priest, 'Father, I have sinned: I'm having a torrid affair with a voluptuous woman of 20.' 'Well, first things first,' says the priest. 'How long since you've been to confession?' 'Actually, I've never been before,' says the 92-year-old man. 'You see, I'm Jewish.' 'Well, why are you telling me?' says the priest. 'Hey,' says the old man, 'I'm telling everybody.'

It was extremely crowded in the supermarket carpark. The old woman spied a park and was just about to turn into it when a young man cut in front of her and took the space. He got out, locked his door and, seeing the old woman glaring at him, jibed, 'Too bad. You've got to be young and fast.' The old woman backed her car up and then drove fast forward into the back of the young man's car, denting it severely. 'Why did you do that?' yelled the young man. The old woman replied, 'Because I'm old and better insured.'

Rules for over-sixties:

1 Never pass a loo without availing yourself of the opportunity.
2 Never trust a fart.
3 Never pass up an erection even if you're on your own.

The young girl's grandmother sat for hours watching the clothes spinning round in the drier. The young girl's friend asked her what her grandmother was doing. 'Well,' said the young girl, 'my granny's lost her glasses, and she thinks she's watching wrestling on TV.'

There's three old ladies in an old folks' home. One says, 'I'd like a man with a dragon on his chest.' The second one says, 'I'd like a man with two dragons on his chest.' The third one says, 'I'd like a man with one dragon on the ground.'

This old guy goes to the doctor. Because his hearing's not all that good, his wife accompanies him. The doctor examines him at some length and then says, 'We'll have to do some tests. I'd like you to go to a medical lab, and I'd like you to take them a urine sample, a faecal sample and a sperm sample.' 'What's he want?' says the old guy to his wife. 'He says he wants your undies,' she replies.

There's a 92-year-old man standing on a street corner and he's sobbing almost uncontrollably. 'Why are you crying,' asks a passerby. 'Well,' says the old guy as he catches his breath, 'I've just won Lotto. The other day I married a 35-year-old, a real beauty, and she can really cook – and we've been making love ever since.' 'Yes, but why are you crying?' insists the passerby. 'Because,' says the old guy, 'I can't remember where I live.'

An old lady was inspecting a big pile of carpets in a showroom. She bent over, and, as she did so, she farted. 'I am sorry,' she said to the salesman beside her. 'That's all right, lady, but you'll shit yourself when you hear the price.'

An old couple about to embark on a second honeymoon decided that a visit to their doctor might be a sensible thing. The doctor gave them a good check-up and put them on a course of iron tablets. Unfortunately, they never got round to the second honeymoon. They both went rusty.

Steptoe and son were on a buying trip to another town, and one night they were caught without accommodation and the only bed they could get was a double. Now young Harold was not very keen on sharing with the dirty old sod, but he had no choice. At two a.m. old Steptoe woke up and said ''Arold, I need a woman.'

'Oh, go back to sleep, you dirty old man,' said Harold.

''Arold, I need a woman very badly.'

Harold sat up and said, 'You can't have a woman for three reasons. One, you're a dirty old man. Two, you're too bloody old. And three, that's my cock you've got hold of.'

Two old maids were sitting up in bed, angry because the house ghost was playing up. One of them said, 'Cut out the hocus and pocus.'

The social worker was going around the wards, and stopped to see if an old patient needed anything. The patient had a bowl of almonds alongside the bed and the social worker looked at him lying there with no teeth and said, 'How do you eat the nuts?' 'Oh, I can't,' said the patient. 'So you can have some, if you like.' The social worker did, and then she remarked, 'Why would anyone bring you nuts when you have no teeth?' 'I don't mind,' said the old chap. 'I rather like sucking the chocolate off them.'

What has 90 balls and makes old ladies sweat?
Bingo.

You know you're old when:
Your little black book contains only next-of-kin.
You get winded playing chess.
You're still chasing women but can't remember why.
You turn out the lights for economic reasons.

You sit in a rocking chair but can't get it going.
You can't stand people who are intolerant.

Three old codgers were sitting on a park bench when a pretty jogger went past. The first old chap said, 'If I was younger I'd jump up and grab her and give her a big cuddle.' The second old chap said, 'If I was younger I'd jump up and give her a big cuddle and then a passionate kiss.' The third old chap said, 'If I was younger I'd jump up and give her a big cuddle and then a passionate kiss, throw her on the ground, rip her shorts off and . . . What was that other thing we used to do?'

An elderly couple were experiencing memory loss, so they started attending classes where they learnt a memory method where everything was recalled by word association. The old fellow was telling his neighbour about this. 'What's the teacher's name?' asked the neighbour. 'Let's see,' said the old fellow. 'What's that flower that smells nice but has prickly thorns down the stem?' 'A rose,' offered the neighbour. 'Hey, Rose,' shouted the old fellow, 'what's the name of the teacher at the memory class?'

It's great to be rich but you need to be young to get the full value from it, as the wealthy old man found out. He proposed to a young lady and she readily accepted. Unfortunately, though the desire was there, the flesh was not willing. The old man spent thousands of dollars on medical cures, but nothing availed. He was told of a juju man in Africa who had helped people like him. So, Africa it was. The witchdoctor readily accepted the case for a fee. The cure was quite simple with the right powders. The witchdoctor warned that it was a powerful cure, and although the old man would only get one erection a year it would last for as long as he wanted it to. 'When you are ready for action just say, "One, two, three," but be warned, it will only work once a year,' said the witchdoctor. 'When you want it to go down, you just say, "One, two, three, four."' Back with his wife, the old chap was about to surprise her. He was lying in bed with her and said, 'One, two three,' and, presto!, he had a daddy of an erection. His wife turned to him and said, 'What did you say, "One, two, three" for?'

ARTHUR OR MARTHA

Martha: 'We're invited to a fancy-dress party. I thought I'd wrap myself in plastic and go as a transparent personality.'
Arthur: 'I thought I'd fill my mouth with custard and go as a zit.'

Three newly released mental patients are digging a hole. Well, actually, one of them is digging it while the other two stand leaning to either side of him. The foreman comes up and says, 'What are you two doing just standing there?' One of the men replies, 'We're lamp posts.' 'You're fired is what you are,' says the foreman, and off the two men go. Then the man who's been digging the hole gets out of the hole and starts to leave as well. 'You don't have to go,' says the foreman. 'Yes I do,' says the man. 'How do you expect me to dig without adequate light.'

First man: 'I didn't sleep with my wife before I was married. Did you?'
Second man: 'I don't know. What's her name?'

What did Helen Keller say when she was handed a grater?
'This is the most violent book I've ever read.'

English lecturer to students: 'Today I'm going to talk to you about Gertrude Stein. That is for those of you who aren't more interested in her daughter Phyllis Stein.'

Roses are red,
Violets are blue,
I'm a schizophrenic
And so am I.

The graffiti originally read I love grils. Someone had crossed out grils and written girls beneath it. Someone else had later crossed girls out and beneath that written No, I love grils.

I looked in the sky and spotted a bird.
The bird spotted me and I wiped my eye.
Birdy, birdy in the sky,
I'm so glad that elephants don't fly.

Pinocchio's girlfriend keeps complaining of splinters in her fanny, so Pinocchio goes to see Geppetto. Geppetto gives Pinocchio some sandpaper and tells him to try it on his dick and to keep rubbing till it's really smooth. A month goes by, and the next time Geppetto sees Pinocchio he says, 'How's your girlfriend?' Pinocchio turns to him and says, 'What girlfriend?'

First man: 'Thanks for the meal. I really enjoyed the chicken. What did you stuff it with?'
Second man: 'Stuff it with? What are you talking about? It wasn't empty.'

A man bought twenty pairs of socks. 'I hope they were all right,' said his friend. 'Well, actually,' the man answered, 'half of them were left.'

The overseer put down his whip and called out to the galley slaves: 'I've got good news and I've got bad news. The good news is that you can take a 10-minute break. So put your oars down and stretch your arms. Have a drink of water. The bad news is that after your break the captain wants to go water-skiing.'

The pilot's voice came over the loudspeaker, cool, calm and confident: 'This is your captain speaking. I've got good news and I've got bad news. The bad news is that we're going to crash because we've run out of fuel. The good news is that I'm going to parachute down to get help.'

The captain's voice came over the ship's loudspeakers: 'This is your captain speaking. I've got good news and I've got bad news. The bad news is that the ship's sinking. The good news is that, in spite of sharks, the water is warm.'

A man was crawling around under a street light when a policeman walked by. 'What are you doing?' asked the policeman. 'I'm looking for my lucky 50-cent piece,' said the man, 'I dropped it along the road there,' and he pointed down the road. 'Well, why are you looking here?' asked the policeman. 'Because the light's not so good along there,' said the man.

This old woman is weaving all over the road. A traffic cop comes along behind her, and through his loud hailer he yells, 'Pull over. Pull over.' The woman stops, and the traffic cop pulls up behind, gets out of his car and walks forward to the woman's car. She winds down her window and casts him a withering glance. She indicates some knitting on the seat beside her. 'It's not a pullover,' she says. 'It's a cardigan.'

A taxidriver picked up a woman one night who was dressed totally in black, and she also wore a pointed hat. As they drove along she asked if the driver could go a bit faster. 'You won't get a ticket,' she said. 'I'm a witch and can get you off anything.' 'Well,' he said, 'if you're a witch, I'd like to see you prove it.' With that she grabbed him by his dick and turned into a motel.

When young Jimmy went to school, the teacher took him to task for his absence the previous day. 'Where were you yesterday, Jimmy?' 'My dad got burnt,' said Jimmy. 'He must have been badly burnt if you couldn't come to school,' said the teacher. Jimmy replied, 'Yes, ma'am. They don't fool around in those crematoriums.'

Ambrose and Rastus worked picking cotton. Ambrose was about to marry Mary Lou who also worked picking cotton, but many miles away. Ambrose and Rastus therefore had a long walk to where Mary Lou was so that the marriage could take place, Rastus serving as best man. On the way back it rained and the three of them had to take shelter in a small cabin that only had one bed. Rastus said he was very tired and there was no way he was going to sleep on the floor after all the distance he had walked to be best man. The floor was a dirt floor and it was wet, so a solution was effected with Rastus and Mary Lou sleeping side by side and Ambrose top-and-tailing with his feet between them. Now, they hadn't been long in bed when Rastus said, 'Why, Mary Lou, what's dat I'se got ma hand on?'

'Oh, Rastus, you naughty boy,' she answered, 'them's ma titties.'

A little while later Rastus said, 'Why, Mary Lou, what's dat I'se got ma hand on now?'

'Oh, Rastus, you naughty boy, that's ma navel.'

A little while later Rastus said, 'Why, Mary Lou, what's dat I'se got ma hand on now?'

And Ambrose answered, 'That's ma big toe, and it's going to stay there all night.'

This bloke had been named by his parents Arthur Penis. When he reached the age of 21 he applied to have his name changed by deed poll. 'What's your present name?' asked the official that he dealt with. 'Arthur Penis,' answered Arthur Penis. 'And what do you want to change your name to?' asked the official. Arthur answered, 'Art Penis, thanks.'

An American politician was touring the Indian reservations trying to get voter support. At the first village he visited he ranted on to the tribe for about an hour, and every now and again they would wave their arms and call out, 'Um boog a goo goo.' All this did was encourage him, and he would promise more and the Indians would keep waving and chanting, 'Um boog a goo goo.' On his way back to his Cadillac the politician remarked to his assistant, 'They certainly liked what I said.' Just as he was about to get into his car, the chief guided him away from standing in a large cow pat. 'Um boog a goo goo,' said the chief, pointing to the crap.

Fred was walking down the street when his best friend Joe pulled up alongside in a brand-new Porsche. 'Where the hell did you get the car from, Joe?' asked Fred in disbelief. Joe said, 'I met this bird at a party last night and we danced the night away. When I was about to ring for a taxi, she told me not to bother; she would take me home. She drove up into the hills, stopped at a quiet place, got out and took off all her clothes. She said, "You can have anything you like." So I took the Porsche.' 'Good thinking, Joe,' said Fred. 'Her clothes probably wouldn't have fitted.'

KNOCK KNOCK

Knock knock.
Who's there?
Dick.
Dick who?
Dick 'em up. I'm tongue-tied.

Knock knock.
Who's there?
Martini.
Martini who?
Martini hands are frozen.

Knock knock.
Who's there?
Olive.
Olive who?
Olive across the road.

Knock knock.
Who's there?
Matthew.
Matthew who?
Matthew latheth are undone.

Knock knock.
Who's there?
Yvonne.
Yvonne who?
Yvonne to be alone.

Knock, knock.
Who's there?
Amos.
Amos who?
A mosquito bit me.
Knock, knock.
Who's there?
Andy.
Andy who?
And he bit me again.

Knock knock.
Who's there?
Madam.
Madam who?
My damn foot's stuck in the door.

Knock knock.
Who's there?
Noise.
Noise who?
Nice tits.

Knock knock.
Who's there?
Cash.
Cash who?
No, thanks, I'd rather have a peanut.

Knock knock.
Who's there?
Irish stew.
Irish stew who?
Irish stew in the name of the law.

Knock knock.
–Will someone please answer the door!

Knock knock.
Who's there?
I don't know.
I don't know who?
I don't know who either.

Knock, knock.
Who's there?
Cows.
Cows who?
Cows don't go who, they go moo.

'WHAT'S A VERANDAH?'

A woman went into a sex shop and asked for a vibrator. 'Certainly, madam,' said the assistant, beckoning the woman with a motion of her index finger. 'Come this way.' 'If I could come that way,' said the woman, 'I wouldn't need a vibrator.'

Teenagers are God's punishment for having sex.

There's three ages of man: tri-weekly, try weekly, try weakly.

Father: 'I found a packet of condoms on the verandah.'
Son: 'What's a verandah?'

In the old officers' club one day, Carstairs turned to Frobisher and said, 'How long since you've had sex?' 'Let me see,' said Frobisher, 'it would be 1945.' 'Good God, man, that long,' sputtered Carstairs. 'Well,' said Frobisher, 'it's only 21:30 now, so that's really not too bad.'

A couple were having some very hot moments in the front seat of the chap's car. His hands were everywhere and so were hers. 'Hop into the back seat,' he said. 'No, thanks,' she said rather coolly. So he sat back and had a cigarette or two until his ardour cooled. But it wasn't long before they were back at it again, and both but all undressed, and he said again, 'Hop into the back seat.' 'No,' she said with quite some determination. 'What the hell's the matter with you?' he said. 'You must want it as much as I do.' 'I do,' said she. 'Well, why don't you get in the back, then?' 'Because I want to be here in the front with you,' she said.

Thor, the god of thunder, came down to spend a day with mere mortals and thought he would like a bit of nooky whilst in his human state. Well, he made out with a young lady who had an impediment in her speech. When it was time to depart back to the heavens, for his leave pass was up, his guilty conscience started to prick, so he thought he'd better tell the young lady who he was. 'I am Thor,' he said proudly. 'So am I,' said the girl, 'but I'm thatithfied.'

When the children returned from their holidays the teacher was interested in what sort of diet they had while they were away. One little chap told how he and his brother and sister had been camping at the beach with his parents and they'd eaten quite a lot of fish and seafood. 'But Mum and Dad,' he went on, 'didn't have the same as us, for just about every night they ate candles.' 'Surely not,' said the teacher. 'You must be mistaken.' 'No, teacher,' said the boy. 'When we went to bed at night, Mum would say to Dad, "Blow out the candle and we'll have a bit."'

A young butcher boy was making a delivery to a house. He knocked on the door, and when it opened there was the most beautiful woman he had ever seen standing there without a stitch of clothing. Her body was fantastic, and the young man just stood there shaking. The woman said, 'Quick, come in and shut the door.' Once he was inside she paraded all her wares and then she said, 'What do you think is the most sensitive part of my body?' The boy said, 'Your ears.' 'How the hell can you say that?' 'You heard me coming, didn't you?'

A young man back from his honeymoon was questioned by his workmate, an older man. 'What was the sex like, son? At it morning and night?' 'Not likely,' said the lad. 'I couldn't even get it in. She was just too small.' 'Oh,' said the learned one, 'I'll tell you what to do, then. Get a breakfast cup, half fill it with Vaseline, dip the old fellow in the cup and then have a prod. Now, if you keep doing this – dip and prod, dip and prod – eventually you will penetrate.' The young man just looked at his workmate in amazement. 'Can you get yours in a breakfast cup?' he said.

The valet came into the duke's bedroom, as was the custom, pulled the drapes open, went over to the bed and said, 'Good morning, sire.' When he pulled the blankets back he noticed a rather large erection. 'I see you have an erection, your lordship. Shall I go and inform the duchess?' 'No,' said the duke, 'not this time, Jeeves. Get me a pair of plus fours and I'll smuggle it down to the village.'

A woman went into a Catholic church and asked the priest if he would preside over her wedding. 'But I must tell you, Father,' she said, 'that although I have been married three times already, I am still a virgin.'

'I don't see how you could have been married three times and still be intact,' said the priest.

'Well, my first husband was a gynaecologist and all he wanted to do was look at it. My second husband was a psychiatrist and all he wanted to do was talk about it. And my third husband was a carpenter and he always put it off till another day. But the man I want to marry now, Father, is a solicitor, so I know I'm going to get screwed.'

This boy came home from school one day and, when his mother asked him what kind of day he had at school, he said, 'Well, it was a big day for me, Mum. Today I had my first fuck.' His mother was somewhat taken aback, and she sent him off to his room to await his father's return from work. Straightaway his father returned his mother sent him up to see the boy. 'I've just heard the news,' said the boy's father as he entered the room, 'and I must say you're a bit of a quick worker. I mean, being just 13 and all . . . So, do you think you'll do it again?' The boy turned to his father and said, 'Maybe. But I'll have to wait till my bum stops hurting.'

A man came home from work one day and said to his wife, 'They're saying that the milkman has slept with every woman in the street but one.' His wife replied, 'I bet it's that snobby bitch in Number 34.'

Little Johnny met his mother at the door after she had been away for a couple of days. 'Guess what, Mummy? Yesterday I was playing in your wardrobe and Daddy came in with the lady from next door, they got undressed and got into bed and he got on top of her and –'

'Stop,' said his mother. 'Not another word . . . Wait till your father gets home. Then I want you to tell him exactly what you've told me.' When his father came home she told him that she was leaving him.

'Why?' he asked in all innocence.

'You tell him what you told me, Johnny.'

'Well,' said Johnny, and told the whole story again. '– and then Daddy you got on top of her and did just what Uncle Bob did to Mummy.'

Little Willie went to the toilet one night and there was a lot of action taking place in his parents' bedroom. He looked in and saw his father donkey deep in his mother. He rushed into the bedroom and climbed on to his father's back for a horsey ride. His father couldn't stop as he was very close to the vinegar stroke. Just then his mother started to groan and call out. 'Watch out, Daddy,' said Little Willie. 'It's about here that the milkman gets bucked off.'

A fellow was drinking with a workmate who kept buying more beers, and of course he had to reciprocate. Time crept on until he realised that he'd be in shit street when he got home. He told his mate of his predicament. 'No problem,' said his mate. 'Have a couple more so you are really late. She'll be long gone to bed. You go straight to the bedroom, get in under the blankets, slip her nightie up and give her oral sex. It never fails.' So the chap went home, snuck into the bedroom, got under the blankets and began. Nothing but female moaning and groaning until the chap was so pushed for a leak that he said he'd be away for a tick, but he'd return in a flash to give more of the same. He went into the bathroom to find his wife there. She had been curling her hair. 'What are you doing in here?' he said. 'Shhh!' said his wife. 'You'll wake up my mother, you drunken lout.'

A chap came over the hill in his new Cadillac, and, lo and behold, there was a couple engaged in sexual intercourse right in the middle of the road! Luckily, the car had ABS braking, and the chap managed to stop inches from the couple. Enraged, he leapt from the car. 'What in hell's teeth do you think you're up to?' he said. The bloke of the couple stood up and said, 'I was coming. She was coming. You were coming. But, praise the Lord, brother, you were the one with the brakes!'

What's the speed limit on sex?
Sixty-eight. Because at 69 you have to turn around.

HISTORICAL

A particular battle between the English and the Scots. One morning, the English general had his troops lined up on a ridge waiting for the mist to clear so he could see the enemy. From the mist-laden gully below came a Scottish voice: 'Any one Scottish soldier can beat any two English soldiers.' This was too much for the general and he sent two soldiers down into the mist. There was a rattle of sabres and then silence. Then a little while later, again that Scottish voice: 'Any one Scottish soldier can beat any 10 Englishmen.' The general selected 10 good men and sent them down. Again there was the rattle of sabres and then silence. Just when the general was about to send more men into the mist, one badly wounded trooper came clambering up to the ridge. 'It's a trap,' he called. 'There are two of them.'

When is a door not a door?
When it's ajar.

Mum was using the binoculars to look over stock on the farm when she spotted Dave giving Mabel a right rogering behind a bush. 'Dad, come and have a look at this,' she yelled. And when he got there she asked him, 'How long have they been carrying on like that?' 'Oh, I don't know,' said Dad, 'but judging by the freckles on his arse I would say all summer.'

Dave and Mabel were sitting on the verandah watching the sun go down and the rams hard at it in the house paddock.

'Gee, Mabel,' said Dave, 'I'd love to be doing that.' 'You can if you like,' said Mabel, 'they're your sheep.'

Dad and Dave and Mum were staying in an old country hotel after being at a cattle show. Mum woke Dad up. 'Listen, Dad, there must be rats in the wall between our room and Dave's.' Dad listened for a while, then banged on the wall and called out, 'Dave, take your bloody cuff links off.'

Dad and Dave had installed modern plumbing in the house, and the time came to blow up the old dunny. They set the charge and, just as it was about to go off, Mum, forgetful as ever, and forgetting they had an internal, came waddling out to the old one. She'd just sat down when it exploded. Dad and Dave rushed over to find Mum laughing. 'What's so funny, Mum?' said Dad. 'It's just as well I didn't let that one go in the kitchen,' she said.

The peanut stood on the railway track.
Its heart was all aflutter.
Along came engine number nine
And turned it into peanut butter.

I eat my peas with honey.
I've done it all my life.
It may taste kind of funny,
But it keeps them on my knife.

Prince Edward was in bed with Mae West, and before they did anything the Prince said, 'You are very fortunate. I have slept with both queens and princesses.' 'Which way do you want me to turn?' asked Mae.

Mae West met Tarzan in the jungle and was very impressed with his body, so while they were sitting around the fire one night she thought, Now is the chance to demonstrate my womanly strength. She casually picked up a coconut and, putting it between her ample bosoms, brought her arms together and cracked it open. Tarzan just said, 'Ugh', and went on stoking the fire with his dick.

1940. Two fellows who were trying to avoid going into the army were attempting to devise a plan so they would fail the medical. The first chap attended his medical and came home elated. 'I failed,' he said, 'and I'm therefore medically exempt from the armed forces. You can do the same next week,' he said, and gave his friend one of the clumsy rupture trusses they had in those days. 'Just put it on and you will fail.'

His mate went into the examination and had his test, and when he noticed the doctor writing down M. E. on his report he said, 'So I'm medically exempt?' 'No,' said the doctor, 'that means Middle East. Anyone who can wear a rupture truss upside-down is fit enough to ride a camel.'

The Second World War. North Africa. A bunch of New Zealand troops, under the command of a somewhat by-the-book major, are coming to terms with the use of the grenade. One among them, Jackie by name, is a stutterer, a very bad stutterer. Well, the major explains to the men that they should pull the pin and count to four, then throw their grenades. 'One,' says the major, and all the men say 'One' along with him. 'Two,' says the major, and right then Jackie hurls his grenade . . . Ka-boom! The others then do likewise. There's panic and pandemonium. 'Kee-rist!' the major addresses Jackie, 'what'd you have to go and do that for?' 'W-w-well,' says Jackie, 'if I'd w-w-waited f-f-for f-f-four w-w-we'd all b-b-be b-b-bloody d-d-dead!'

During the air raids in London a couple were charged with having sex in a public place. 'I was having sex with my wife,' was the man's plea. 'Why didn't you tell the constable,' asked the magistrate, 'when he apprehended you in the act?' 'It was so dark at the time I didn't realise,' said the man.

A soldier came home from the war on a troopship and was met by his loving wife. As they had to wait until the next day to get a train back to their home town, they spent the night in a hotel. They drank a lot and had a great reunion in bed. When the man awoke in the morning, feeling very seedy, and saw a woman beside him in the bed, he thought he'd better leave her some money. 'How much do you want?' he said. The woman yawned and said, 'Twenty bucks will do, honey, and leave some chewing gum for the kids.'

This story goes back to the olden type grocery store, where you told the grocer what you wanted and he ran around like a scalded cat filling your order. This story even goes back to when the till was just a drawer under the counter . . . It was a quiet day and the grocer's wife was cleaning around under the counter. Her arse was sticking in the air and the grocer became very aroused. They finished up having it off on the floor behind the counter. Just as the grocer got to the vinegar stroke a customer came in. The grocer leapt up and shoved his dork in the till. The customer said, 'You're looking very pleased with yourself.' The grocer replied, 'Well, um, yes. I've just come into money.'

You remind me of a man.
What man?
The man with the power.
What power?
The power of hoodoo.
Who do?
You do.
I do what?
Remind me of a man.
What man?
The man with the power . . .

A tip for the trots – Epsom salts.

What's old and wrinkled and smells of ginger?
Fred Astaire.

Order in the court,
The judge is eating beans.
His wife is in the bathtub,
Shooting submarines.

Beans, beans, the musical fruit –
The more you eat, the more you toot.

One fine day in the middle of the night,
Two dead men got up to fight.
Back to back they faced each other,
Drew their swords and shot each other.

Would things have been different if Khrushchev had been assassinated rather than Kennedy?
Yes, Aristotle Onassis wouldn't have married Mrs Khrushchev.

Lyndon Johnson and some friends were once motorboat riding in the Florida Everglades, with a black manservant in attendance. God looked down and saw arrogance and privilege and water skis. He shouted down, 'Give the black man a go on the water skis.' The black man was set in the water to ski behind the boat. 'What a bossy bastard,' said one of the men, referring to God. 'Yes,' said Lyndon Johnson, 'but what he doesn't know about hunting crocodiles . . .'

Mary had a little lamb,
It had a touch of colic.
She fed it brandy twice a day,
And now it's alcoholic.

Berlin, 1968. This guy had just woken up after a hectic night with a German girl he'd met, and seeing that he was feeling good he offered her some US dollars. 'Nein dollars, nein dollars,' she said. 'Marks, please.' Now, this is where his ego took over, and he thought, I must have been superb if she doesn't want dollars. I'll be generous, he thought, and he gave her eight out of 10.

THIS WAY, THAT WAY

Two old women are sitting talking. One says to the other, 'Now, my Frank, you know, he always drank too much tea, tea when he woke up, tea just before he went to sleep, tea all day long. And I always said to him, "It'll kill you drinking that much tea." But he wouldn't listen to me.' And the other woman said, 'And that's what killed him, I suppose.' 'No,' said the first woman. 'He was crossing the road and got run over by a truck.'

This young guy walks into a chemist and the assistant says, 'Can I help you?' The young guy says, 'Yes. I'm looking for a decent deodorant.' 'Ball or aerosol?' asks the assistant. 'Armpit, actually,' says the young guy.

There's this crim and he buys a brand new Mitsubishi and he paints one side of it white and the other black, half white, half black, right down the middle. His mate says to him, 'Why're you doing that?' 'So's I'll never get caught again leaving the scene of the crime,' says the crim. 'If there's ever any witnesses, they'll see different cars.'

There's this guy in this car with his wife, and late one night on the way home from a party he runs a red light. Before he knows what's happening he's pulled over by a traffic cop. The cop says to him, 'Do you realise you just went through a red light?' 'Oh, no I didn't,' says the guy. 'Oh, yes you did,' says the cop. 'Oh, no I didn't!' says the guy. 'Jesus,' says the cop; and then addressing the guy's wife he says, 'Is he always this argumentative?' And the guy's wife says, 'Only when he's drunk.'

A lawyer, a nun and an Irishman go into a pub. There's a mouse sitting on the piano playing a little violin. The nun turns to the Irishman and says, 'This is the weirdest joke I've ever been in.'

After a long sleepless night a man confronted his next-door neighbour: 'Did you hear me banging on the wall last night?' 'No, I didn't,' said the neighbour, 'but that's all right. We were having a bit of a do ourselves and I probably couldn't hear you over the noise.'

This kid gets home from school one day and he says to his mother, 'Where do I come from?' 'You'll have to wait till your father gets home,' says his mother. 'He'll explain it to you.' After a while his father comes home and the boy says to him, 'Where do I come from?' 'Well,' says his father, and he launches into a long speech about the birds and the bees and how Mummy and Daddy . . . But the kid interrupts and says, 'Where do I come from? There's a new boy at school, you see, and he comes from Hamilton.'

This chap's off work. One day, two days, three days . . . And then the boss rings him up, and goes, 'I see you're still off work.' And the guy goes, 'Yes, well, I'm pretty sick.' And the boss goes, 'How sick are you?' And the guy goes, 'Well, I'm in bed with my sister.'

Two workmen had just finished laying a 12 x 12 metre carpet and there was a lump in the middle of it. 'Oh, those must be my cigarettes,' one of the workmen said. 'I wondered where I'd left them.' So, instead of ripping the whole carpet up, he got out his mallet and hammered the lump flat. Just then the lady of the house came in and said, 'I've brought you some tea, and this packet of cigarettes that one of you must have left in the kitchen. Oh, and by the way, have either of you seen my little boy's hamster?'

Two men were sharing a cabin on a ship. After their first night at sea, one man woke and went to get dressed, but he couldn't find his clothes. He shook the other man awake and said, 'Have you seen my clothes?' The other man said, 'When I came in last night your clothes were sprawled all over the chair so I bundled them up and put them in the little cupboard.' 'Which little cupboard?' asked the first man. The other man sat up and pointed to the porthole.

There was this man called Fred. He was standing outside the ferry building ripping up bits of newspaper. After a while, one of his mates came up and said, 'Hey, Fred, what are you doing throwing bits of newspaper around?' 'Keeping the lions away,' said Fred. And his mate said, 'But there's no lions around here.' Fred answered, 'I know. It just goes to show how well it works.'

A man goes into a butcher shop and says to the butcher, 'Excuse me, but I was wondering, do you have a pig's head?'

'No,' said the butcher, 'it's just the way I part my hair.'

'I don't want to go to school, Mum.'

'You've got to go.'

'But I hate it at school.'

'You've got to go.'

'But it's really terrible. I hate the place. The teachers are mean to me and the kids are always picking on me.'

'You've got to go. After all, you are the headmaster.'

A sheriff walks into a saloon and says to the barman, 'I'm looking for a man.'

'What's he look like, sheriff?'

'He's wearing brown paper trousers, a brown paper shirt and a brown paper hat.'

'What's he wanted for?'

'Rustling.'

I was watching TV and a commercial came on saying if you have a video and a scanner you can slip the scanner along the time code and that will make sure you record whatever it is you want to record. So I decided to play a little trick. I got a packet of laxatives and slipped the scanner across the bar code, and the video recorded *Baywatch*.

When the customer approached the counter to buy a ticket, the cinema ticket seller said, 'But, sir, that's the tenth ticket you've bought.'

The customer looked at her and said, 'Yes, I know, but there's a man at the door who keeps tearing them in half.'

There's these guys sitting down having lunch, three guys, and there's a ring ring ring, you know, *ying ying, ying ying*. And the first guy holds his hand up to his ear with the thumb and little finger outstretched and goes, 'Yes, hello? Yes, right . . . Okay, see you later . . . Okay.' And the third guy goes, 'Shit! That's amazing. How do you do that?' And the first guy points to his head and says, 'There's a receiver in there.' A few minutes later there's another *ring ring*, and the second guy, *without* holding his hand up to his ear with the thumb and little finger outstretched, goes, 'Yeah? . . . Yeah, okay . . . yeah, yeah.' And the third guy goes, 'What was that?' The second guy says, 'The same. A telephone call . . . It's built into my head; it's all built in. You don't have to have a telephone or anything.' Then the third guy suddenly stands up, leaning slightly forward, with his legs apart, just like he's going to shit, and goes, '*Oooh aaaah oooh eeeh.*' 'My God, what's the matter?' says the first guy. The third guy answers, 'I think there's a fax coming through.'

They've just discovered rice on the moon. And you know how many rice dishes you can make? Well someone's opened a rice restaurant on the moon. And the food's really nice, but there's no atmosphere to speak of.

Three vegetables were walking along the road, a lettuce, a cucumber and a tomato. Tomato fell behind, and Lettuce and Cucumber stopped. Cucumber, who'd been growing increasingly impatient with the pace of their progress, went back to Tomato and jumped up and down on him, yelling, 'Ketchup, you bastard.'

A blind man decides to go parachuting. So he arranges everything, and he even takes his little white dog along, though he's on an extremely long leash. The jumper before him says, 'Is this your first jump?' 'Yes,' says the blind man. 'Well, there's one thing I'd like to know,' says the other jumper. 'What's that?' says the blind man. 'How do you know when to pull the ripcord?' 'That's easy,' says the blind man. 'When the leash goes slack.'

The young vicar of the village proposed to and ultimately married the prettiest and most virtuous girl hc could find. The first night of the honeymoon was also going to be his first experience of sex, and he was extremely nervous. After having a sumptuous dinner at their hotel the couple were walking through the lounge when the vicar turned to his bride and said, 'You go on up, darling. I won't be long.' So she went off to their room while he dallied, fretfully. After 10 minutes or so he took a deep breath and ascended to their room. He took another big breath at the door, and then he went in. His wife was lying on the bed with a very flimsy nightie on. 'Oh, my goodness,' said the vicar, 'I thought you'd be on your knees.' 'Okay,' said his wife, 'we'll do it that way, but I warn you it gives me hiccups.'

It was a quiet summer evening on the reservation, and as was the custom the tribe sat round the chief's wigwam and listened to his words of wisdom. It was question and answer time, and the chief as he smoked his pipe would ponder each query and then give a very full and complete answer. 'Almighty chief,' spoke one brave, 'among your extensive powers you have naming rights for each baby born on the reservation, but surely sometime you will run out of names.' 'Not so, my son,' answered the chief, 'for when a baby is born I call on Nature to give me inspiration. For example, the other morning when that baby girl was born the sun was shining on the river, so I called her Sparkling Dawn. A fortnight ago when the last little boy was born the night was very dark, so I called him Grey Night . . . Tell me, Two Dogs Fucking, why do you ask?'

Two young lads were playing marbles outside a house of ill fame. They were very observant and noticed that each customer that came along knocked at the door three times and then a voice from behind the door would say, 'Who sent you?', and the man would say, 'Joe sent me.' 'How much have you got?' the voice would go on, and the man would answer, 'Twenty dollars.' Then the door would open and the man would be admitted. After a while the boys became more inquisitive as more customers came and went. Finally they pooled their resources and found they had $1.50. 'Let's have a go,' said one of them to the other. So they knocked three times at the door. 'Who sent you?' 'Joe sent us.' 'How much have you got?' 'One-fifty.' The door opened and a bouncer grabbed them, banged their heads together and threw them back out on the road. They picked themselves up and one of the boys said, 'Thank God we didn't have $20. We couldn't have stood any more of that.'

An undertaker who also happened to be a city councillor was a bit pushed for time. He had a council meeting this particular night, plus he had just prepared two bodies for interment the next day. He still had to wait for one of the deceaseds' wives to come along and view her spouse's body in the coffin. Well, it had all gone wrong. The bodies were to be buried on the morrow, as I said, but somehow the wrong suits were on the wrong bodies. The apprentice boy was the only one of the staff still on duty, so the undertaker offered him three hours overtime to swap the clothing on the two corpses. Twenty minutes later, as the undertaker was about to enter the council building for a meeting, the boy went past on his motorbike. The next morning the undertaker said to the boy, 'How did you do the job so quickly?' 'Easy,' replied the boy, 'I just swapped heads.'

There's these two chaps who get on a train, a rather Colonel Blimpish sort of chap – with a bowler hat, rolled umbrella, that sort of thing – and this rather down-at-heels tramp. They end up sharing the same carriage. The train sets off, and after a while the tramp gets off his seat and squats on the floor and shits. And it stinks. *Whoo-eee!* The other fellow – the Blimpish chap – lights a cigar, hoping thereby to neutralise the smell. He's puffing away, and the tramp, by now reseated, says, 'Put it out. Put it out. Can't you read the sign?' And the other fellow looks up at the wall where the tramp is pointing and sees there's a No Smoking sign.

This fellow was turned away from a knocking shop. He did not have enough money. But the madam did offer him the opportunity to enter that week's jackpot for $1,000. His eyes lit up. 'I'll be a starter,' he said. 'Well,' said the madam, 'we have a fairly big room in there, and a chook, and to win the prize you have to chase the hen until you catch it. All the time you must have your donger in your hand. If you catch the chook you get the $1,000. And if you can successfully have sex with the fowl there's another $1,000 in it for you. There is a time limit of 10 minutes.' The fellow couldn't resist, but when it came to it he failed.

A week later he called again, but again he didn't have enough money, though what he did have was just enough to gain admittance to watch a lesbian show. Oh, well, any old port in a storm, he thought to himself. He was ushered into a room where there was a small grandstand with a lot of men watching two women perform through a two-way mirror. 'Wow,' he said to the bloke alongside him, 'what a show.' 'Yeah, but you should have been here last week,' said the bloke, 'they had some stupid bugger trying to stuff a chicken.'

A commercial traveller broke down on a stormy night and found a haven with an old farmer and his very pretty young wife. Food was at a premium, however, as the farm was not going all that well. The wife made some scones, which were just about all scoffed. The young wife had been giving the traveller the glad eye and, when the old man went to bed, she blew out the candle and said, 'Quick, now's your chance.' And the traveller jumped up and grabbed the last two scones.

A very pretty and shapely young lady on holiday at a very flash hotel found that the roof was an ideal place to sunbathe. So each day after some shopping she would go up to the roof and bask in the sun, with her bathing suit on, of course. On the third day, it was so private that she slipped out of her togs, but being a very decent and respectful person she lay on her stomach and pulled her towel over her posterior. She was just on the point of dozing off when she heard someone running up the stairs. It was the assistant manager. 'Excuse me, madam,' he said. 'We, um, ah . . . we do not mind you sunbathing in your swim suit, as you did on the other days, but, I mean, naked, well . . .' 'What difference does it make?' said the young lady. 'I am covered with a towel.' 'Yes, but, madam, you are lying over the dining-room skylight.'

Bill the Bastard was about to be sentenced. 'What have you got to say for yourself?' said the judge.

'Fuck all,' said Bill.

'What did he say?' the judge asked the clerk.

'He said fuck all, your honour.'

'I must be going blind,' said the judge. 'I was sure his lips moved.'

◎ ◎ ◎

TALL TALES

For his eighth birthday the boy's father bought him a pet from the pet store. It was a rare animal from the edges of the Gobi Desert, a rary. The baby rary was green and had three eyes, and was as cuddly as a kitten and as friendly, but after a couple of weeks the rary had started to grow at an alarming rate. Soon it was as big as a full-grown cat. Not long after it was the size of a medium dog. The boy's father went to the pet shop but the owner didn't know how big a rary grew, this being the only one they had ever had. By the time it was six months old the rary was the size of a small cow. And it ate and ate and ate. By the time a year had passed the rary was as big as a buffalo and growing still. Finally, in exasperation the boy's father said to him, 'I'm afraid we'll have to get rid of the rary. We can't afford to feed it any more, and it'll soon be so big that we'll have nowhere to keep it. You must take the rary to the cliff by the sea and push it over.' The young boy cried and protested and refused to carry out his father's wishes. But finally he succumbed, realising that the rary would soon be as big as an elephant. So, one sad day he put a rope around the rary's neck and led it to the cliff, which was nearby his home and, looking down at the sea, gave the rary a gentle shove. The rary dug his feet in and refused to budge, and looking at the boy said, 'That's a long way to tip a rary.'

This boy crosses the border every day. Every day he goes through the customs checkpoint with his little red wagon

and every day the customs officer checks in the little red wagon. He looks through comics and lengths of string and odd bits and pieces, and every now and then the boy's dog is in the little red wagon. Day after day the customs officer searches the little red wagon, sure that the boy is smuggling something, but day after day he finds nothing. One day the boy stops crossing over the border. A while later the customs officer happens to run into the boy at a supermarket. 'I'm sure you were smuggling something,' says the customs officer. 'I was,' says the boy. 'I was smuggling little red wagons.'

There were once three friends. One was a snail, one was a slug and the third was a centipede. One day they were watching their favourite TV programme. They were thirsty, so they looked in the fridge for some Coke. But there wasn't any Coke. So Slug and Centipede told Snail to go and get some Coke. But he said, 'You guys will be dead by the time I come back.' Slug's excuse was, 'I'll get stuck to the ground.' So Centipede said he'd go.

Two hours later . . . Snail and Slug noticed that Centipede wasn't back, and they became worried and decided to go and look for him. When they opened the door, there he was, just outside the door. They asked him, 'Where's our Coke?' 'Hey,' he replied, 'I'm still putting on my shoes.'

This guy meets this gorgeous blonde and he really wants to impress her. So he takes her out to the most high-class and expensive restaurant in town. He orders the most expensive dishes on the menu. He orders the most expensive wine. But, unfortunately, the woman doesn't seem too impressed. Then the floor show comes on. It's Tom Jones. At a break the guy excuses himself and goes backstage and gains admittance to the dressing room. 'Tom,' he says, 'I've always been your biggest fan, I've got all your records, I catch you in concert whenever I can. I wonder if you'd be so kind as to do me a really big favour.' Well, Tom Jones is pretty taken by this and says, 'Sure, I'll do whatever I can.' So the guy says, 'What I'd really like you to do is to come across to my table after you've finished and say gidday to me, like we're old friends. That'd really impress this woman I'm with.' 'Sure,' says Tom, 'By the way, what's your name?' 'Fred,' says the guy. And he goes off. Tom Jones finishes his set, and then, instead of going backstage, he mingles with the diners, slowly making his way to Fred's table. When he gets there he looks at Fred and does a double take. 'Fred,' he says, 'old buddy. Long time, no see. How're you keeping?' Fred, seeing how impressed his girl is, says, 'Oh, go on, Tom, fuck off, can't you see I'm busy.'

There's a man called Carruthers, a decent sort of chap, but a bit of a snob and a frightful social climber. After years of intense networking, and flattery and downright obsequious behaviour, he was finally invited to the Worthington's Christmas banquet, the social event of the year. He'd lately done an advanced etiquette course, and incidentally a course in witty repartee, and fancied that he could handle any sticky social situation with aplomb. The entrée and main courses passed without incident, but as a waitress dished something dessertish for the man next to him a tit sprung out of her rather too tight top and plopped into a largish bowl of custard. To create a diversion Carruthers yelled, 'Everyone, look out the window.' All heads turned as one. Quick as a flash Carruthers whipped out his handkerchief and mopped the protruding tit and popped it back into the woman's top. He then noticed that everyone was staring out the window still and turned to look. He saw two dogs fucking on the lawn.

This guy was mucking around on his computer. He'd just got on the Internet, and he was so excited that he stayed up all night visiting various sites. About five o'clock in the morning he was in a chat room, and one of the characters asked him if he liked dogs. 'Yes,' he answered, 'I like dogs.' The next thing he knew the police were breaking down his door and screaming, 'Where's the dog fucker? Where's the dog fucker?'

A drunk man. He comes out of this building where he's been. He's walking down the street, singing away to himself, humming away, staggering along, and he's got this little yellow dog on a string, it's just trotting along beside him, a squat little yellow dog. And about two blocks away this other guy's walking his Alsatian, a large, thoroughbred Alsatian, massive, black-haired; striding along, macho man and his massive Alsatian, choker chain, *beautiful* dog. Sees the drunk with the little yellow dog, hails him from afar and says, ''Scuse me, sir, think you'd better take a left down there, keep your little dog away from mine. Cross the street. This dog is an attack dog, trained to kill. I don't want to have any trouble with you, please, sir.' The drunk goes, 'Ahrgh, get fucked.' This drunk lurching along the road, 'I'll walk anywhere I like.' 'Please, sir' – they're getting closer – 'Please, sir, I don't want any trouble. This is serious.' By this time the Alsatian was straining at the choker. The drunk goes, 'Get your pathetic dog off the footpath.' The little yellow dog's just squat on the footpath, just trotting along, not looking either way, just trotting along, this strange little yellow dog, very low to the ground, squat, trotting along. The Alsatian gets a bit closer. 'Not sure that I can hold him back, sir.' The Alsatian: 'Grrrrrr!', pulling on the chain, really going berserk. Drunk's saying, 'Oh, ya big poofter, keep away from my little dog.' The big Alsatian, he can't hold him any longer, lunges forth. 'I told you, you silly old bastard.' It lunges toward the little yellow dog, teeth clashing, ready to attack. The little yellow dog rears back, clamps his jaws on the Alsatian's front leg, severs it, leg falls off. Champ on his other leg, *champ, champ, champ*, smashes this Alsatian to pieces, chomps him up, chomps him into little pieces. The Alsatian's just lying on the ground. There's a stunned silence. The drunk's saying, 'I told you, you fuckwit, I told you.' The guy's stunned. He's saying, 'Ah, what! My poor Alsatian. What a terrible thing. What sort of dog is it? . . . What sort of dog is that?' The drunk says, 'I don't know what sort of dog he is, but before I cut his tail off and painted him yellow he was an alligator.'

It was a few days ago. There was, in the queue outside the Casino, some kind of domestic incident between a man and his wife. And he was drunk, and I heard, one person said that he was hitting her, and the other person just said it was a domestic incident, so he didn't say whether he was hitting her or not, but there was some kind of nasty scene and the police were called. And the police approached this guy and he ran off, he ran, I think it was, all the way up Victoria Street, and then down, left down Hobson Street, and the police chasing him all the way. And then he saw an open door, so he jumped in the door, and ran up some stairs and through a room and then found a wall panel that was off, and so he jumped into this cavity and crawled along and he was in the air-conditioning ducts in the Casino. And just being held up by the ceiling tiles, which of course gave way, and he fell down into the staffroom cafeteria where the security staff was sitting round having their lunch, or their dinner, landed on the table they were all sitting at in front of the 20-stone head of security who picked him up, put him on the ground and sat on him till the police came.

This guy goes into a bar and there he meets a farmer who's offering $500 to anyone who can make his donkey laugh. The guy takes up the bet and accompanies the farmer outside to where the donkey is. He approaches the donkey and leans toward him and whispers something in his ear. The donkey bursts out laughing. 'How did you do that?' asks the farmer. The guy just smiles and taps his nose on the side. 'Okay. But before I give you the $500,' says the farmer, 'why don't you give me a chance to win it back? I bet you $500 you can't make the donkey cry.' For a second time the guy takes up the bet, but stipulates that the farmer must shut his eyes. The next thing the farmer knows the donkey is crying and crying, big donkey tears rolling down his cheeks. 'You win,' says the farmer. 'Here's your $1,000. But won't you please tell me how you did it?' 'Easy,' says the guy. 'The first time I told the donkey that my dick was bigger than his, and he burst out laughing. The second time, I showed him, and he burst out crying.'

There was a young inventor who invented a new type of racing cycle, and he was sure it would revolutionise track and road racing. However, he did have doubts about the ability of the frame to withstand high speeds. He had a friend with a Mustang who agreed to tow him at high speed to test the machine. After they'd hooked up, the inventor said, 'I will ring my bell once if I want you to go faster, twice if I want you to maintain speed, but I'll ring it repeatedly if I want you to slow down.'

With that they were off, with the Mustang getting up to 60 and the bike handling well. Then along came a black Corvette. The driver of the Mustang forgot the bike and a drag race began. A traffic cop got them on his radar screen and radioed into headquarters. 'There's a Mustang and a Corvette racing down Highway 26,' he said, 'at 105 mph, and, I'm not kidding, there's a cyclist behind them ringing his bell and wanting to pass.'

WAITER, WAITER

'Waiter, waiter, there's a fly in my soup.'
'That's all right, sir, he won't eat much.'

'Waiter, waiter, there's a fly in my soup.'
'Would you like a spoon?'

'Waiter, waiter, how do you serve shrimps?'
'We bend down, sir.'

'Waiter, waiter, how long will my spaghetti be?'
'About fifteen inches, sir.'

'Waiter, waiter, you've got your thumb in my soup.'
'That's all right, madam, it's not hot.'

'Waiter, waiter, this food isn't fit for a pig.'
'I'll take it back and find you some that is, sir.'

'Waiter, waiter, there's an awful film on my soup.'
'What do you expect for two dollars – *Lawrence of Arabia*?'

'Waiter, waiter, there are flies playing on my plate.'
'They have to practise, sir. They're playing in the cup next week.'

'Waiter, waiter, there's a slug in my mince pie.'
'I think it's fat, sir.'
'I know it is – it's eaten all the pastry.'

'Waiter, waiter, there's a fly in my soup.'
'It's possible. The cook used to be a tailor.'

Waiter: 'How did you find your steak, sir?'
Customer: 'I looked under a mushroom, and there it was.'

'Waiter, waiter, I didn't order this.'
'But you said you wanted something different, sir.'

There was a man who ate a lot of foods that were rich in iron. As time went on that was all he ate. Finally he ate nothing but silverbeet, which is very rich in iron. One day he went into a fancy restaurant and ordered a large plate of silverbeet. He ate it up and then he ordered another. He ate that one all up as well. The waiter came over with the cheque. The man stood up. He burped and nailed the waiter to the wall.

WHY DID THE CHICKEN CROSS THE ROAD?

Why did the chicken cross the road?
Why not?

Why did the chicken cross the road?
It didn't.

Why did the chicken cross the road?
Because it wanted to.

Why did the chicken cross the road?
Because it had nothing better to do.

Why did the chicken cross the road?
Because its car was parked on the other side.

Why did the chicken cross the road?
Who cares?

Why did the chicken cross the road?
For some foul reason.

Why did the chicken cross the road?
To show the opossum how it's done.

Why did the chicken cross the road?
Winston Peters: I will have my people get to the bottom of it and if an inquiry is necessary we will have one.

Why did the chicken cross the road?
Jim Bolger: I agree with Winston.

Why did the chicken cross the road?
A Consultant: Deregulation of the chicken's side of the road was threatening its dominant market position. The chicken was faced with significant challenges to create and develop the competencies required for the newly competitive market. We convened a diverse cross-spectrum of road analysts and best chickens and, along with one of our highly paid and skilled facilitators with deep skills in the industry, organised a two-day retreat with other senior management chickens in order to leverage their personal knowledge capital, both tacit and explicit, and to enable them to synergise with each other in order to achieve the implicit goals of delivering and successfully architecting and implementing an enterprising wide-value framework across a continuum of poultry cross-median processes. The meeting was held in a park-like setting, next to a lake, enabling and creating an impactful environment which was strategically based, industry focused, and built upon a consistent, clear and unified market message and aligned with the chicken's mission, vision and core values. This was conducive towards the creation of a total business integration solution that will better enable the chicken to successfully 'merge' with the oncoming traffic.

Why did the chicken cross the road 15 times?
Because his overalls were stuck to the street light.

Why did the chicken cross the playground?
To get to the other slide.

Why did the turkey cross the road?
The chicken was on vacation.

Why did the hedgehog cross the road?
Because he was tied to the chicken.

Why did the hedgehog cross the road?
To visit his flatmate.

Why did the hedgehog cross the road?
To show what it was made of.

Why did the hedgehog cross the road?
To show that it had guts.

Why did the turkey cross the road?
To prove he wasn't a chicken.

Why did the chewing gum cross the road?
Because it was stuck to the chicken's foot.

Why did the dinosaur cross the road?
Because chickens weren't around then.

Why did the rooster cross the road?
Because it was the chicken's day off.

Why didn't the elephant cross the road?
It didn't want to be mistaken for a chicken.

Why did the pervert cross the road?
Because he had to get to the hospital to have the chicken removed.

Why did the psychic cross the road?
To get to the other side.

Why did the 50-year-old cross the road?
For no real reason.

Why didn't the chicken cross the road?
I don't know.

DO YOU KNOW THE ONE THAT GOES . . .?

A baker immigrated from Italy many years ago and had a fairly successful business until the bigger bakeries came out with sliced bread. His accountant said, 'You will need to get a slicer to compete.' After a hunt he found a loaf slicer, but it wasn't productive enough; it would only slice one loaf at a time. Then he bought another loaf slicer, but that wasn't productive enough; it would only slice two loaves at a time. Then one day his luck changed – he found a four-loaf cleaver.

Two Kiwis working on the Woomera rocket range away back in history were finding the outback rather an isolated spot. The whole area where they were was under a liquor ban, for safety reasons, and it meant a trip of several hundred miles just for a beer. One day while putting the fuel into a rocket, one of them spilt a couple of drops on his hand, and without thinking he licked them off. A little while later he had his mate try some too, for he was getting high on it, better than any moonshine he'd ever had. By the end of the day they had consumed more than just a few drops, and they both retired to their cabins early. Next morning the phone went and, when the first chap answered it, it was from his mate. 'Have you farted yet?' said his mate. 'No.' 'Well, I did, and I'm making this call from Singapore.'

There was a young man from Trace
Who projected a fart into space.
What with cosmic attraction
And celestial contraction
It backfired and blew shit in his face.

Two missionaries in Africa were captured by very hostile cannibals, who put them in a big pot of water and started a fire underneath. As the water got hotter one of the missionaries started to laugh. 'What's so funny,' said the other one. 'We are being boiled alive. They are going to eat us.' 'Well, the joke's on them,' said the first missionary, 'I've just peed in the soup.'

Two patients were escaping from an asylum. They'd got to the top of the outer wall and discovered they had no rope and it was a long way down. But they did have a torch. One said, 'I will shine the torch down and you can slide down the beam.' 'Do you think I'm stupid?' said the other. 'You'll wait till I'm halfway down and then you'll switch it off.'

Long ago, when sailing ships ruled the waves, a captain and his crew were in danger of being boarded by a pirate ship. As the crew became frantic, the captain bellowed to the first mate, 'Bring me my red shirt.' The skipper put his red shirt on and they repelled the invaders, with only a few casualties. When they were sailing again in clear waters, the captain broached the rum and they all had a chin-wag. One nosy crewman had to ask the captain, 'Why do you always wear a red shirt when you're going to do battle?' 'If I am wearing a red shirt,' said the captain, 'and get wounded, the red shirt won't show the blood, and you men will think I'm okay and will continue to fight unafraid.' The next morning the lookout screamed, 'Two pirate ships on the port side.' 'Get me my red shirt,' called the skipper, 'and my brown pants.'

At a particular factory it was noticeable that the boss was sneaking off early each day. It wasn't long before the crew had worked out a system where, in an orderly fashion, one or another of them would take some time off when the boss went AWOL. When Neil's turn came he went home and snuck in to surprise his wife. It was a surprise, because he came across his boss performing chesterfield gymnastics with his wife. When Neil's turn for time off came again, he wouldn't go. 'Don't spoil it for everyone else,' the boys pleaded. 'No way,' said Neil. 'I almost got caught last time.'

The LAPD, the FBI and the CIA were all trying to prove that they were the trumps when it came to catching criminals. A think-tank institute decided to test them by releasing a rabbit into a forest. The CIA went in and placed informants everywhere. They questioned all mineral and plant life for a month. They couldn't find the rabbit. They concluded that rabbits didn't exist. The FBI went in. After two weeks they had no leads. They burnt the forest, killing everything in it, including the rabbit. They made no apologies. The rabbit had it coming. The LAPD were the last on the job. They went in and came out two hours later with a badly beaten raccoon. The raccoon was yelling, 'Yes, yes. I admit it. I'm a rabbit.'

In the concentration camp the commandant announced that for Christmas there would be a change of underclothes for everybody: 'Hut A will change with Hut B. Hut C will change with Hut D.'

WORD PLAY

Once upon a time an airplane full of Datsun parts ran into trouble in the air. As a result, and in an effort to lighten the plane, the pilot decided to jettison some of the cargo. A farmer standing in a field beneath watched as all sorts of mechanical pieces fell from the plane. 'I'll be damned,' he muttered, 'it's raining Datsun cogs.'

'My wife's gone on holiday, to the Caribbean.'
'Jamaica?'
'No, she went of her own free will.'

The scene is a courtroom. A witness is giving evidence and describes the man on trial as having been 'as drunk as a judge'. The judge interrupts and says, 'Don't you mean "as drunk as a lord"?' The witness answers, 'Yes, my lord.'

This boy scout is going round the neighbourhood offering to do odd jobs to raise money for his scout troop. He knocks at one house and a man answers the door.

'Are there any jobs you want done?' asks the scout.

'As a matter of fact, yes,' says the man, and he goes back into the house and returns with a bucket of paint and a brush. 'I'd like you to go out the back and paint the porch,' he says to the scout, 'and I'll give you $50.'

Two hours later the scout knocks on the front door. He's dripping with sweat and his clothes are spattered with paint.

'I've finished it,' he says when the man answers, 'and, by the way, it wasn't a Porsche, it was a Mercedes.'

Try these tongue twisters:
Oh, if these lips could lisp.
She sells sea shells by the seashore.
Sister Susie sits sewing socks for soldiers.

Then try these tongue twisters:
Slimy slugs sip cider.
Ten teething tigers say terribly tough tongue twisters.
I saw Esau sitting on the see-saw.

Roy Rogers, the famous American film star and country and western singer, was on tour, and to keep everything spick and span he'd bought the very latest in cowboy boots. One night at a hotel in Arizona he left them outside his door to be cleaned for the next morning. When he got up in the morning and fetched them in they had been chewed by a cat and Roy was anything but happy. 'Find the culprit,' he said, 'or I'll sue.' A while later the manager knocked on the door. Roy opened it to find him holding a cat. The manager said, 'Pardon me, Roy, this is the cat that chewed your new shoes.'

An Indian chief had three wives, all of whom were pregnant. Wife one, who slept on a deer skin, had a son and the chief was very happy. Wife two, who slept on a buffalo skin, also had a son, and the chief was very happy. Wife three, who slept on a hippopotamus skin, had twin sons and the chief was over the moon. It must be a sign, he thought, and he went to the heap big medicine man. The medicine man was happy as it proved old ancestor Python in the Grasses' theory that the output of the squaw of the hippopotamus is equal to the sum of the output of the squaws of the other two hides.

A man walked into a bar and said, 'Free rum for Captain Morgan.' The barman ignored him. The man thumped the bar and repeated, 'Free rum for Captain Morgan.' 'If you're Captain Morgan,' said the barman, 'where's your buccaneers?' 'Underneath my bucken hat,' the man replied.

A radio announcer had to present a programme of Rimsky-Korsakov, but he had great difficulty saying the name. All that would come out was Rips Her Corsets Off. So he practised and practised until he got it right. Came the night, he said, 'Ladies and gentlemen, tonight we have a programme of Rimsky-Korsakov's music, and we start with his famous piece, "The Bum of the Flightful Bee".'

A new fish shop started up directly opposite another fishmonger and the owner was a smart dick. When the old shop owner painted 'Flounder' on his window the new chap painted 'Our flounder are flounder.' When the old shop owner painted up 'Snapper' the new chap painted 'Our snapper are snapper.' The next day the old shop owner painted up 'Soles'.

A wealthy lawyer retreated for several weeks each year to his summer home in the backwoods of Maine. One summer he invited a Czechoslovakian friend to come and stay. The friend, happy to get anything free from a lawyer, agreed. They had a wonderful time.

One day, however, they were up early picking raspberries and blueberries for their breakfast when they were approached by two large bears, a male and a female. The lawyer noticed them in time and ran for cover. His friend was not so lucky. The male bear knocked him down and ate him up. The lawyer rang the sheriff, who rushed out with his high-powered rifle. The bears were still there. 'He's in that one,' said the lawyer, pointing to the male. The sheriff took aim and shot the female. 'What did you do that for?' exclaimed the lawyer, 'I told you he was in the other bear.'

The sheriff just looked and said, 'Do you really think I'd believe a lawyer who said the Czech was in the male?'

When Quasimodo, the Hunchback of Notre Dame, was about to retire, the church officials were interviewing applicants for the job. Each applicant was sent up into the tower with Quasimodo, who would show them how to ring the bells, and the officials would be on the street below to judge the sound. An Irishman climbed all the way to the top and watched as the Hunchback jumped on to the bell to get it swinging. 'Sure, that will be no trouble at all,' he said, but he was a little shy about jumping the gap to the bell, so he used a piece of wood to give the bell a shove, and as it came back closer to the edge where he was he jumped. But alas, too soon, and he hit the bell with his head and fell hundreds of feet to the road below. The body was splattered on the ground, and someone said, 'Who is it? It's not Quasimodo.' Someone else said, 'I don't know who it is, but his face sure rings a bell.'

A teacher asked the pupils in his class to enumerate the essentials of life. Billy Smith stood up and said, 'Air.' Sadie Brown stood up and said, 'Water.' Mary Cunningham stood up and said, 'Food.' Henry Cobald stood up and said, 'Fanny.' The teacher was very irate and gave Henry a note to take home to his father. The next day he asked Henry, 'Did your father give you a thrashing last night?' 'No, sir,' said Henry. 'We talked about it, and Dad thinks you must be a bit of a wanker.'

The Indian Prime Minister was touring Europe, and at a concert one night he heard the Vienna Boys Choir. He thought they were brilliant, and asked his secretary to get as much information as he could about them, because India needed ambassadors like those lads, all around the world. 'The only difference,' said the Prime Minister, 'is that I'd like a much bigger group.' The secretary did a good job, and had 500 boys brought together for training, but no matter how hard they tried they couldn't get the boys to sing soprano as required. The secretary conveyed to the Prime Minister that the problem was that Indian boys reached puberty earlier than their Western counterparts. The only way to get high voices was to castrate the whole 500. 'Do it,' said the by now obsessed leader. They did. It was successful. The boys are now known as the Indian Knackerless 500.

When Beethoven passed away, he was buried in the local churchyard. A couple of days later the town drunk was passing the burial plot and he heard some strange sounds coming out of the mound. Terrified, the drunk ran and got the priest. The priest listened and became just as scared as the drunk, so he ran and got the town magistrate. The magistrate arrived and put his ear to the mound and listened. 'It's music,' he declared and listened some more. 'Ah, yes, it's Beethoven's Ninth symphony being played backwards.' He listened for a while longer. 'There's the Eighth symphony and it's backwards too. Most puzzling.' So the magistrate kept listening. 'There's the Seventh . . . Sixth . . . Fifth. My fellow citizens, there is nothing to worry about. It is only our friend Beethoven decomposing.'

Little Johnny was frantically waving his arms in the classroom. The teacher said, 'What's the trouble, Johnny?' 'I need to take a piss, teacher.' Before she let him leave the room, the teacher told Johnny that the word to use was 'urinate', and when he came back he was to have thought up a sentence using that word. When he came back, the teacher said, 'Okay, Johnny, give me your sentence.' Johnny said, 'Urinate, but if you had bigger tits you'd be a nine.'

A small guy went into an elevator which was already occupied by a huge dude. The big guy noticed this fellow looking him up and down. 'I am seven feet tall,' said the big guy. 'I weigh 350 pounds, I have 30-inch biceps, a 12-inch penis and each of my testicles weighs a pound.' He held his hand out and said, 'My name is Turner Brown.' The little fellow fainted. The big dude picked him up and revived him and asked, 'What's wrong with you?' The small guy said, 'Excuse me, what did you say before?' The big guy repeated, 'I am seven feet tall, I weigh 350 pounds, I have 30-inch biceps, a 12-inch penis, each of my testicles weighs a pound and my name is Turner Brown.' 'Thank God,' said the small guy, 'I thought you said turn around.'

The maharaja of an Indian province had been on a trip to England, where he'd been very impressed by the Duke of Edinburgh and his World Wild Life scheme. When he got home he decreed that no more tigers were to be killed. It wasn't long before the place was overrun with tigers. So many people were getting eaten that the population threw the maharaja out of office. It was the first time on record where the reign had to be cancelled because of the game.

Once upon a time there were seven short bachelors who lived in the same house. They owned their own home, and a diamond mine, and they were very happy together. They whistled while they worked and they sang a happy song as they went to and from their work. Upon the scene came a very pretty girl, one Snow White, and she shifted in with them. Now on a ship this would have been bad luck. And in a soap opera it would have been good for 20 episodes at least. Did Snow White moving in upset these lads' equilibrium? No. And why not? Because they were fucking Dopey.

The man stumbled and banged into the door. His friend was with him and said, 'Have you had your eyes checked?' 'No,' answered the man, 'they've always been blue.'

There are two sausages in a pan and one says to the other, 'Golly, it's hot in here.' The other one says, 'Oh, wow, a talking sausage!'

'Howdy, cowboy, what's your name?'
'Tex.'
'Where're you from?'
'Louisiana.'
'So, why are you called Tex?'
'Would you want to be called Louise?'

First man: 'You bin is full of toadstools.'
Second man: 'How do you know that?'
First man: 'Because there's not mushroom inside.'

First man: 'I used to play the elastic trumpet.'
Second man: 'Where?'
First man: 'In a rubber band.'

First man: 'I've decided to invest all my savings in 1996 calendars.'
Second man: 'Why? 1996's been and gone.'
First man: 'Because if 1996 ever comes back, I'll make a fortune.'

CORN

The Lone Ranger and Tonto had been riding the range all day when they stopped for a rest. They were extremely hungry. The Lone Ranger turned to Tonto and said, 'Tonto, there's a hill up aways and beyond it a valley, and through the valley runs a stream, and by the side of the stream, about a mile along, there's a bacon tree. Why don't you ride along there and get some bacon while I start a fire.' 'Okay, kemo sabe,' said Tonto, and off he went.

Time passed, and the Lone Ranger was beginning to get worried as Tonto hadn't returned. But just then he heard a noise, of a galloping horse, and looking in the direction of the hill he saw Tonto riding closer! And as he came closer, the Lone Ranger saw that Tonto was cut and bleeding and shot full of arrows. 'What happened?' called the Lone Ranger. 'It wasn't a bacon tree,' said Tonto, 'it was a hambush.'

Three men are standing on top of a very tall building. One of them says, 'I bet I can drop my watch from here and then run down the stairs and get to the street just in time to catch it.' The other two egg him on. He takes his watch off, holds it out and lets it go. Then he turns and runs, over the rooftop to where the stairs are, and then quickly down the stairs. Down many flights of stairs. Down, down, down, until he reaches the bottom floor. He runs out through the building's front doors and is *just* in time to catch his watch.

Now the others think they'll give it a go, so the second man drops his watch off the top of the building. Then *he*

runs down the stairs, but he's faster than the first man, and by the time he gets to the street he's got enough time to do a handstand and a forward roll before stopping to catch his watch.

Now it's the third man's turn. He looks over the side of the building, takes his watch off and, like the others, lets it go. Then he walks slowly across the rooftop to the stairs, and then slowly walks down all the flights of stairs to the bottom. He walks out on to the street, gets in his car and drives to his house. He goes in and, as it's dinnertime, he has his evening meal. Then he gets in his car and drives back to the building, where the other two men are standing waiting for him. He stops the car, gets out and stands on the pavement, puts his hand out and catches his watch. 'How did you do that?' asks one of the other men. 'Easy,' he says, 'it's a stop watch.'

There's this programme on the radio, and it's to do with knock knock jokes. It's on every week, and every week they give a prize for the best knock knock joke of the week. And towards the end of the year they have semi-finals and then a final, and then a grand winner is chosen who gets an all-expenses paid trip for two to the south of France. This one year a contestant showed up who introduced himself as Bedgood White. He was a flamboyant dresser with a penchant for cravats, and he fancied himself as a master of witty repartee.

Now, contestants had to go through a screening process to make sure they would be okay on the air, and this was basically a matter of an underling getting them to start off and follow through on a knock knock joke and see how they responded as the joke progressed. So the underling eyed up Bedgood when his turn came and told him to say knock knock. 'Knock knock,' said Bedgood. 'Who's there?' said the underling. 'Gert,' said Bedgood. 'Gert who?' said the underling. 'Gert fucked,' said Bedgood White. 'Well, I'm sorry,' said the underling, 'but you just won't do. We can't have that sort of language on the air.'

The next week, however, Bedgood was back, though this time in disguise. He had on a false beard and had dyed his hair. He finally reached the front of the screening queue. The underling told him to say knock knock. 'Knock knock,' he said. 'Who's there?' said the underling. 'Ah,' said Bedgood. 'Ah who?' said the underling. 'Ah, fuck you,' came the reply. Again Bedgood was sent away.

He brooded. If only he could get on the programme. Because he was, without any doubt at all, one of the greatest knock knock people on the planet, being, as he was, a master of witty repartee. He was born for the programme. To be the grand winner was his destiny. So he decided on a plan. Disguising himself again, this time in dark glasses and a handlebar moustache, and with his hair cut very short, he went to the next week's screening. 'Knock knock,' he said, after being primed by the underling. 'Who's there?' the underling replied. 'Arthur,' said Bedgood. 'Arthur who?' said the underling. 'A thermometer,' said Bedgood, a tactical move and one exercised with considerable restraint. Well, the underling was pretty impressed by this. 'Okay,' he said, 'you're on the show.'

So the next night Bedgood showed up in his disguise to go on the air. And he was extremely excited. This was it! The breakthrough! The point towards which he had laboured for so many years. He'd give them what for! He'd show them witty repartee! So he's on the air with the host. Finally it's his turn. Bedgood says, 'Knock knock.' And the host says, 'Who's there?' Bedgood says, 'Sigsimundo.' The host says, 'Sigsimundo who?' And Bedgood says, '*Fuck off.*'

GOTCHA!

A man has just started up in business as an actors' agent. At 10 o'clock in the morning on the first day in his new office there's a knock on the door. Thinking it must be a client, he leans forward on his desk and picks up the phone and starts talking urgently into it: 'Hi, Bob,' he says, 'about that contract . . .' and so on. Over his shoulder he calls, 'Come in.' The door opens and the man outside comes in while the actors' agent keeps talking into the phone. He holds up his finger to the man who's come in to indicate he'll just be a minute, but he talks on for about five minutes more. When he's finished he slams the phone down, turns to the man who's come in and says, 'Those producers can be difficult at times, but I sure sorted him out . . . Now, what can I do for you?' And the man who's waited so patiently says, 'I'm from the phone company. I'm here to hook up your phone.'

Mary had a little lamb
And some chunks of meat.
She put them in her sandwich,
She thought it was a treat.
She chewed them up so very well,
And said, 'Vegetarians can go to hell.'

There's this old sailor gets on a bus, and he sits down in the only vacant seat, next to a young punk. After settling himself, he takes a good long stare at the young punk. Then a while later he takes another long stare at the punk. And then again.

Finally, the punk's getting tired of being stared at and he says, somewhat aggressively, to the old sailor, 'What's your problem? Haven't you ever seen a punk before?' And the old sailor says, 'It's not that. It's just that I fucked a parrot once, and I wondered if we were related.'

Bill Gates dies and goes to . . . the big screening desk in the sky. And Saint Peter's there and he says to Bill Gates, 'Okay, now you're dead, you get to go to heaven or hell. But your case is rather a difficult one. On the one hand there's the PC, but on the other hand there's Windows 95. I think I'd better let you make the choice. So why don't you check them both out . . . Go over there into that viewing room and check out the promotional material.' So Bill Gates goes and does this. He watches this film on heaven, and it's clouds and angels and everybody's rapturously happy and so on, but it all seems a little bit boring. So he checks out the film on hell, and it's full of fast cars and beautiful women and all the attractions of sin. And Bill Gates thinks, Hey, this doesn't seem too bad at all. So he goes back to Saint Peter and he says, 'Look, if it's okay with you I think I'd really prefer to go to hell.' 'Fine and dandy,' says Saint Peter and – *whoosh!* – Bill Gates is in hell. As the mist clears, though, he becomes aware that he's crucified on a cross with all kinds of little demons clutching at him and poking him with pitchforks, and when he looks down all he can see are vile seething snakes. 'What's the story?' he says. 'Hell wasn't supposed to be like this.Where's the women and fast cars?' And Saint Peter answers him, 'That's promos for you.'

The time: Ancient Rome. The place: the Mediterranean. A galley cuts through waves on its way to North Africa. Conditions on board are sweltering, and all of a sudden one of the galley slaves drops dead. The overseer pulls him out of the way and then proceeds to lay about all the other galley slaves with his lash. 'It's a tradition,' he says, 'that when someone dies we have a whip around.'

There's this guy and he's a cigar connoisseur and he buys these absolutely top-drawer Cuban cigars. And because they're so valuable he insures them against theft and everything else, like flood damage, fire and so on. But then he smokes the cigars. And he enjoys them immensely. The next day, however, he lodges an insurance claim to the effect that the cigars have been destroyed by fire. Obviously, the insurance company isn't too happy, and things end up in court. After a long, sweaty day the court finds in his favour. But as he leaves the court, this guy, he's arrested for arson.

A guy, who had figured out a ruse to rip off his insurance company, went to court in his wheelchair and claimed $50 million from the insurance company because he'd lost the use of his legs in a workplace accident. The insurance company was suspicious of the guy and thought they'd set out to prove that he was faking. It did no good. The judge awarded the guy the $50 million. As he was wheeled out, the lawyer for the insurance company approached him. 'You won't rest easy,' he said to the guy. 'We'll observe you, wherever you are, and one day we'll prove you were faking.' 'Fine,' said the guy. 'I'll give you my itinerary. I'm going to the Ritz in London, then on to Cannes, then I'm going to take a quick whizz around the Mediterranean in a helicopter. You're welcome to follow me. Oh, and then I'm going to Lourdes.'

This young chap, eager as all get-out, goes into a chemist's shop and buys three packets of 12 Durex. The chemist serves him, though all the while giving him a somewhat hostile eye. That night the young chap goes to his girlfriend's for dinner; it's to be a big night as he's going to meet her folks. He gets there and knocks politely at the door; his girlfriend answers and takes him into the sitting room. Then she leaves the room and comes back with a man to whom she's saying, 'I'd like you to meet my boyfriend, Daddy.' Her father comes into the room, and the young chap sees that he's the chemist!

It's been raining heavily, and a lawyer and a doctor are driving, in separate cars, one behind the other, along a narrow country road. The lawyer stops his car on the side of the road and gets out to relieve himself. The doctor rounds the corner, starts to skid, slams on his brakes and slides into the back of the lawyer's car, knocking it further off the road. He gets out. 'Well, anyway, look's like there's not much harm done,' he says to the lawyer, who walks over to him while putting a cell phone away, 'but you could've parked off the road a little bit more.' 'Whatever,' says the lawyer, and then he adds, pulling out a hip flask, 'Would you like a drink?' The doctor accepts the flask and has a hearty swig. Then he hands the flask back to the lawyer, who puts it away. 'Aren't you going to have a drink?' enquires the doctor. 'Not yet. I'll wait till after the police get here,' says the lawyer.

Once upon a time in a Middle Eastern kingdom two men where arrested for plotting against the king. When they were brought before him he was enraged with them and said, 'As a punishment you two will lose your manhood, and you will lose it according to your occupation.' To the first man he said, 'What do you do?' The man answered, 'I'm a butcher.' 'Oh, well, then,' said the king, 'you shall be castrated with a cleaver.' Then he turned to the second man and said, 'What do you do?', and the second man replied, 'I'm a lollipop maker.'

A forester out walking through thc trees came across a fellow with his arms around a tree and handcuffed besides. His trousers were around his ankles. 'What's going on here?' enquired the forester. 'I was going through the forest,' said the man, 'when I saw this man putting his arms around the trees and making notes. Being nosy, I asked what he was doing. He explained that by putting his arms around the trees he could measure their cubic content, and he offered to show me how to do it. Then it became my unlucky day, because he put these manacles on me and had his evil way. It must be the unluckiest day of my life.' The forester unbuckled his belt and said, 'It sure is.'

This guy in the US gets stopped for making an illegal right turn. As the traffic officer wrote him out a ticket the guy said to him, 'Why don't you shoot me? You've got a gun. And that's what they do in America, isn't it – shoot people for making illegal right turns?' 'Don't be stupid,' said the traffic officer. 'This is America, we don't shoot people for making illegal right turns.' But the guy kept arguing the point and finally the officer was forced to arrest him. So the next day the guy was up in front of the judge and he said to the judge, 'Look, get it over with. Why don't you dispense with this charade and just take me out and shoot me? That's what they do in America to people who make illegal right turns, isn't it?' The judge said, 'Don't be stupid. This is America. We don't shoot people for making illegal right turns.' A tremendous row ensued and the result was that the judge ended up sending the guy to prison. The first night he was in prison, however, the guy attempted to escape and they shot him.

A young matelot was at sea for the first time, on a sailing ship. They had been at sea about two weeks when he said to another Jack Tar, 'It's a bit lonely without a woman, and I think it's going to get worse.' 'It's not bad when you know what to do,' said the Jack Tar. 'Please tell,' said the youngster. 'Tonight,' said the other sailor, 'at six bells, go up to the anchor locker, first of all making sure that there's no one there. There's a barrel in there with a knot-hole in the side. Poke your dick in there and you'll find relief.' The next day the young sailor said to the old sailor, 'By golly, that was good. Can I go back again tonight?' 'Sure, sure.' For three nights he went there, but when he asked to go again the old seaman said, 'Not tonight, son. It's your turn in the barrel tonight.'

Little Dolly was offered 20 cents by the boys to climb up a tree. She was so excited that she told her mother as soon as she got home. Her mother got angry and said, 'You must not do that again. Those naughty boys only want to look at your panties.' The next day she came home with another 20 cents. Before her mother could get fired up, she said, 'Mummy, I didn't let them see my panties. I took them off first.'

An elderly woman went into a bank and wanted to open an account with five million dollars. She felt that with such a large deposit she should meet the manager. She was escorted upstairs to his office.

'How do you come to have so much money?' asked the manager. 'Was it an inheritance or did you make it on the stock market?'

'Neither,' said the woman. 'I gamble.'

'As in horses or casinos?'

'Nope. I bet on people.'

The manager was confused, so she said, 'I'll give you an example. I will bet you that by 10 a.m. tomorrow you will have square balls. I am so sure of this that I am willing to bet $20,000 that I'm right.'

This is too good to be true, thought the manager, and he readily accepted the wager.

The next morning, at exactly 10 a.m., the woman walked into the manager's office accompanied by a man.

'Good morning,' said the manager, full of confidence. 'I am afraid, madam, that you have lost the wager.'

'Not so quick,' she said. 'I will have to see for myself. Don't be shy. This man is my lawyer and he is here to see that the play is fair.'

The manager didn't blink an eye. This was the easiest money he had ever made. He dropped his tweeds and his undies and said, 'There you are, still the same old shape.'

The woman put her hands around his nuts and held them. 'You are the winner,' she said.

Her lawyer put his hands to his head and then collapsed in his chair. The manager fetched him a glass of water. 'I've been done,' he said. 'You see, she bet me $100,000 that she would have you by the balls this morning.'

A guy was sitting at a bar enjoying a beer when a really great-looking woman sat down beside him and gave him a gorgeous smile. He was thinking out his opening line when she jumped up and called out, 'Your apartment? Absolutely not!', and stormed off down to the other end of the bar. The fellow sat there totally confused. She must be a mind reader, he thought. A little while later the woman returned. 'I must apologise,' she said. 'I'm a student doing a study on people's reactions when they are taken by surprise.' The bloke turned to her and said, 'What? $100 for 30 minutes? I don't think so.'

Mr Newly Rich bought a Rolls-Royce, his first, and he talked of nothing else. One day after a round of golf, he gave another member of his club a lift back into town. With great aloofness he said to his passenger, 'I bet you've never ridden in a Rolls before.' 'Well,' said the passenger, 'I admit it's my first time in the front seat.'

A guy walked into a bar and ordered five shots of the most expensive whisky. He lined them up and down they went as fast as possible. The barman said, 'You must've been in a hell of a hurry.' 'You would be too,' said the guy, 'if you had what I have.' The barman said, 'What have you got?' 'No money.'

DIDN'T YOU KNOW?

A spaceship landed adjacent to a service station in the wee hours of the morning. The captain sent his first officer out to interview some of the Earthlings. The first officer went up to a petrol pump and said, 'Take me to your leader.' But nothing happened. Back on the spaceship he told the captain that the Earthlings wouldn't talk, they just stood there with a silly look on their faces and their pricks stuck in their ears.

Little Martin was four years old. One day when he was pestering his mother, she said, 'Why don't you go over the road and watch the builders work. You might learn something.'

Martin was gone for two hours, and upon his return his mother asked what he had learned. 'Well,' he said, 'first you put the goddam door up and when the son of a bitch doesn't fit you have to take the bloody thing down and shave two fanny whiskers off the side, then you have to put the shit of a thing back up.' 'You just wait till your father gets home,' is what his mother said. When his father did get home and Martin related what he had learned, his father said, 'I'll teach you how to behave. Go and get a switch.' Martin said, 'Get stuffed, that's the electrician's job.'

A couple met, and the woman became very interested when the man said he was into kinky sex. 'I'm a starter,' she said. Back to his pad they went, straight in the door and then they got all their gear off. 'Now,' he said, 'I want you to get up on the top of the wardrobe.' He helped her up and then passed her up a bucket of water. 'Okay, we're away,' he said. 'And what I want you to do is this. I want you to flick the light switch on and off, at the same time kick the door, flick water down on me and make noises like a stormy wind.' She did all this while he lay on the floor and wanked. When he finished and lay back to relax, she said, 'When am I going to get a go?' 'What are you talking about?' he said. 'On a night like this?'

A travelling salesman arrives at a house and knocks at the door. A 10-year-old boy opens the door. He's holding a beer and smoking a big fat cigar. 'Is your mother home, little boy?' asks the salesman. The boy flicks ash on the carpet and says, 'What do you think?'

A man and his wife were invited to a fancy-dress party, and the only costume they could hire was an old pantomime cow suit. They went to the party with the man in the front of the cow suit and his wife in the rear. On the way home, when they were no longer in costume, their car broke down and they had to walk across some paddocks, as a short-cut to where they lived. There were cows in the paddock, and they thought it would be amusing to get back into the costume and try to fool the cows. They had not gone far when there was a roar from the bull. 'What's that?' said the wife, who couldn't see out of the rear of the costume. 'It's a bloody great bull,' said the husband. 'What are we going to do?' said the wife. Her husband said, 'Well, I'm going to eat some grass, but I think that you're going to have to brace yourself.'

[Tell whoever you tell this to to close their eyes.] Imagine you're standing in a wide green field. Up ahead is a bit of a rise. All of a sudden you hear a noise: voices and the clanking of metal. A figure appears over the hill. A gnarled, misshapen goblin all done out in leather and studs and brandishing a deadly looking sword. Then another appears, and then another. You see that there are about 30 of these evil killer creatures, and they're after you. You're scared. Will you run or stay and fight? . . . Actually, the goblins don't exist.

This very successful businessman went to the specialist because of continuous headaches. After every conceivable test the specialist told him that it was pressure from his testicles that was the cause of his troubles, and castration, severe as it was, would relieve the strain going through to the base of his spine. The businessman weighed up the consequences of no sex against continuing to make lots of money. The money won. After the operation the man was headache free and he decided to go out and buy himself some new clothes to celebrate. The tailor sized him up, ran the tape around him and got the vital measurements. 'What about a new hat?' said the tailor.

'Sure,' said the businessman.

'That'd be a seven and a half.'

'How could you tell?' said the businessman. 'You didn't measure.'

'It's my business to know,' said the tailor. 'Your new shoes should be, let me see, nines.'

'Right again,' said the businessman.

'What about underclothes?' said the tailor.

'Sure,' said the businessman.

The tailor said, 'You will need 36-inch waist underpants.'

'No,' said the businessman. 'I wear size 34. I've worn size 34 for years.'

'That's not good for you,' said the tailor. 'They'd be too tight on your testicles and give you headaches.'

A guy phoned home from work. A strange woman answered. The guy said, 'Who is this?'

'This is the maid,' came the reply.

'We don't have a maid,' he said.

'I was hired this morning by the lady of the house.'

'Well, this is her husband. Is she there?'

'Um, she's upstairs in bed with someone I thought was her husband.'

'I see . . . Look, you are going to be out of a job, but how would you like to make $100,000?'

'What do I have to do?'

'Go into my study and get the gun from my desk. Then go upstairs and shoot them both.'

There was silence, and then the guy heard two shots. The maid came back on the line. 'What'll I do with the bodies?' she said.

'Throw them in the pool.'

'What pool?'

'Uh, is this 865 7594?'

A man is sitting in a bar when President Clinton comes on TV. 'That man is a horse's arse,' said the man. A man sitting nearby got off his stool and went up to the man and punched him, then turned on his heels and left. A little while later Mrs Clinton came on TV. The man said, 'That woman is also a horse's arse.' Another patron got off his stool and went up to the man and punched him, then turned on his heels and left. The man got off the floor and said, 'This must be Clinton country.' 'Nope,' said the barman. 'This is horse country.'

President Clinton's walking along this track somewhere, wherever, and he comes across a lamp, and he rubs it. And a genie pops out and says, 'You've got one wish, so what's it going to be?' President Clinton rubs his chin for a bit and then says, 'How about world peace?' The genie furrows his brow and says, 'Too hard. Even for me . . . Is there anything else?' President Clinton says, 'How about putting an end to these sex scandals?' And the genie replies, 'On second thoughts, let's give world peace a try.'

Why does President Clinton wear undies?
To keep his ankles warm.

The burglar was having a good night until he heard someone say, 'Jesus is watching you. You'll be sorry.' He lay low for a few minutes so he could determine where the voice came from. There was a squawk, and he realised that he was up against a parrot in a cage. When the parrot repeated, 'Jesus is watching. You'll be sorry,' he spoke to it. 'Hello, Polly, who's a pretty bird?' The parrot replied, 'My name is Cecil.' 'What senseless bugger would call a parrot Cecil?' asked the thief. 'The same senseless bugger that called the Rottweiler Jesus,' said the parrot.

At the end of the year the pupils gave their teacher little gifts of appreciation. The first gift was a box from the florist's son. The teacher held it aloft and said, 'I think these are flowers.'

'That's right, teacher,' said the boy. 'How did you know, teacher?'

'Just a guess,' she said.

The next present was a smaller box from the sweet-shop owner's son. The teacher held the box aloft and said, 'I think these will be chocolates.'

'That's right,' said the boy. 'How did you know?'

'Just a guess,' she said.

The next box was a bigger box from the wine-maker's daughter. The teacher held the box aloft and as she did she noticed a leak in one corner which she wiped with her finger. Then she put her finger to her mouth, licked it with a look of great wisdom and said, 'This must be a Cabernet.'

'No,' said the girl.

The teacher had another taste. 'Could it be a Riesling?'

'No, it's a puppy,' said the girl.

On his fourth visit to the AA meeting the man turned up drunker than a skunk. The secretary was dismayed and said it was a shame. Three times he come sober and it had made them all happy. 'Now the lapse,' he said. 'What brought this binge on?' 'It was my turn to be happy,' said the drunk.

A fellow on a cruise ship was hanging over the rail after only two hours at sea. Another passenger remarked, 'Weak stomach, old chap?' 'Weak be damned,' said the man. 'I'm throwing it as far as anyone.'

GOLF

A widow and a widower met at a golf tournament and, after that, started to see more of each other. Their only problem was that they lived miles apart and wanted to be together. The man proposed that they get married. The woman readily agreed, providing her sons were happy with the idea. The widower met with the sons and told them of his financial situation – he had his own home, a boat, a modern car and some stocks and shares, so they didn't have to worry about him being a gold-digger. 'What about sex?' said one of the sons. 'Infrequently,' said the suitor. 'Is that one word or two?' said the other son. 'That's a question you'll have to ask your mother,' came the reply.

A professional giving a lesson to a lady golfer went to show her the proper swing action. He got behind her and put his arms around her. Unfortunately, the zip on the front of his trousers caught up with the zip on the back of her slacks. After an unsuccessful struggle he had to frogmarch her back to the clubhouse. All was well until a dog came out and threw a bucket of water over them.

Smith and Brown were buddies, playing partners and the best of friends. Smith was 18 stone, Brown was eight. One day whilst playing a friendly, Smith dropped dead. It was several hours before Brown arrived at the clubhouse carrying Smith. Everyone was amazed at the little man's strength. He waved such thoughts away. 'It wasn't strength,' he said. 'He was

my friend. But I must admit that picking him up and putting him down after every shot was quite hard going.'

A man playing with friends one Sunday morning completely lost his cool. He threw his clubs in the lake and stood banging his head against a tree until he dropped unconscious to the ground. The ambulance arrived and he was loaded aboard while his friends stood, caps in hand, looking most unhappy. Just as the driver was shutting the door the man revived, sat bolt upright and said, 'Same time next week, chaps.'

Two old-timers were playing on the Waiheke Island Country Club course and were just about to hit off on the seventh tee, which is adjacent to the main road.

A cortège came past on its way to the cemetery, a hundred yards beyond the seventh green. One of the old fellows took his hat off and held it to his chest. 'Well, give me a 50-foot putt! I have never known you to be sentimental about anything. As a matter of fact, I didn't think you had any feelings,' said the other old fellow. The first old fellow answered, 'It's the least I can do for my wife.'

One sunny day in Dunedin on the Chisholm Park Golf Club course an old fellow climbed up from the clubhouse with his walking stick. The three golfers on the first tee thought he was just an old codger out for a walk. They waited for him to go past, but he approached them and said, 'Do you chaps mind if I play along with you?' 'Where are your clubs?' one asked. 'I manage to get around playing with my walking stick,' he said. The golfers gave each other the let's-humour-him look and away they went. However, the joke was on them.

By the time they had reached the Lawyer's Head, one of the most magnificent golf holes in New Zealand, there was a hold-up, and they had time for a little chat. 'You certainly play good golf using that walking stick. Do you do everything the hard way?' one of the golfers asked the old fellow. 'It doesn't have any interest to me, doing things the easy way, and once I've mastered a situation I usually look for a way to make it more interesting.' One fellow couldn't contain himself and had to ask, 'Do you have any children? And, if so, how did you make that more difficult?' 'Standing up in a hammock wasn't exactly easy,' said the old fellow.

He had separated from his wife. He was so unpopular that even his teenage kids wouldn't borrow money from him. The firm he worked for had him on probation and he was the manager! His temperamental problem was all because of an extremely fierce will to win at golf. His last resort was a visit to a head-shrinker. Professor Nutzinmay had a good reputation when it came to golf freaks who had slipped over the edge. After some discussion and some couch work our bloke was ready to put his new control to the supreme test and return to the course. The Professor said he should go out to the course very early in the morning, take no clubs, but play the whole course in an imaginary round. At no time was he to get excited. He arrived early, but unfortunately there was another golfer, dressed to the nines, already there. Neither wanted to start, so they both stood fidgeting, pretending they weren't interested. The other fellow didn't have any clubs, and before long the penny dropped that they'd both been to the same shrink. They had a little chat and came to the conclusion that things might be even better if they played together in a non-competitive manner. Away they went in the best of spirits, never playing out of turn, even giving putts. When they arrived at the eighteenth both were 17 under par on their imaginary cards. 'You go first, old chap,' said the other bloke, ever so nice, so our bloke stood at the tee, had a practice swing, went back to his imaginary bag and made an imaginary change of clubs, and had a look to check the distance. He put a phantom tee in the ground with, of course, a phantom ball and performed a beautiful swing, his hand over his eyes to shade the sun and watch the flight of the ball. 'There you are,' he said, '231 yards left of centre.' The other bloke went through the same procedure, shading his eyes as well, and said, 'There you are, 232 yards left of centre.' When they reached their balls the first golfer went through his rigmarole and hit a seven iron, as he thought, just past the pin. 'You bloody beaut! I've just holed out for an eagle two. Beat that!' The other fellow just shook his head, pointed to an imaginary spot on the ground and said, 'Like hell! You've just played the wrong bloody ball.'

The Archbishop of Canterbury was having a round of golf with the lady Moderator of the Methodist Church in a charity rally. Neither was a golfer of any ability, but they felt they should do their bit. The Primate, after several non-counting air shots, began to lose his cool, and each time he missed it was 'Damn!', then as the misses increased so did the fury and the bad language. The Moderator smiled sweetly, but when the Primate got to 'Shit! Missed again!' she protested and warned him that the Good Lord was listening and would demand retribution. He may even strike him dead. This fear of God did not worry the Primate, as he was fairly high up the batting list himself. He said 'Shit!' twice more and there was a gigantic roll of thunder and then lightning and the Moderator was struck dead. From up in the clouds came a loud grumble. 'Shit! Missed again!'

There is some very nice veteran's play on Ngamotu, that beautiful course in New Plymouth, and it can be said that a good round on these links is a good round. This particular day an old golfer left the course, went down the hill to the main highway, only got half a mile and his car broke down. Being not far from Fitzroy, where the garage he usually went to was, he thought he would hitch a ride. Not many people stop these days, but just when he decided to walk back to the clubhouse an MG stopped. The driver of this sports car was a young lady with short hair, who was wearing a leather jacket and a white scarf, which hung around her neck and down her back. The old-timer was very happy to accept the lift, and expressed his thanks. With a screech of tyres the young woman took off, passing cars on the inside, on the outside, foot hard down. The old fellow was beside himself. At Bell Block he saw a friend and said, 'Pull in,' and grabbed the opportunity to get away from the demon driver. 'Stop over there behind that truck if you would, please. My friend there can help me.' The brakes went on and with a four-wheel slide the young woman pulled in two inches from the deck of the truck. There was the smell of burning rubber, oil and grease and everything else that makes a smell in an emergency stop. 'Smell that,' said the driver, 'that's living!' 'Smell it,' says the old fellow, 'I'm sitting in it.'

An Irishman playing in the Wednesday morning haggle scored a hole in one, his first. There was great jubilation among his foursome and promises of much drinking at the end of the round. When things quietened down the Irishman was conscious of a movement on his shoulder. He tried to brush away the irritation, but away it would not go. He could hear a little voice and, lo and behold, he saw a little green man sitting there! 'Hello, there. I'm Ace Hole Leprechaun. I'm in charge of holes in one and as you've just scored one you may have a wish.' Now Paddy was conscious that the other fellows did not believe in the little people, so it was a matter of making a quick decision and getting on with the golf. 'Well,' he said quietly, 'as there is nothing worse than a golfer seemingly talking to himself, let's make it quick. I've always been a bit short when it comes to my old fellow, so a bit of an increase would be a bonus.' 'Granted,' said the little man, and then he disappeared. Paddy kept playing, and soon he noticed a warm feeling around his groin, then he felt a spurt of growth, until there was quite a bulge down his thigh. I hope it stops soon, he thought, but it didn't, and soon the lump was below his knee, when finally the growing stopped. Now, it was becoming hard to walk, let alone play golf, so he made the excuse to his partners that he was not well and would have to stop. He gave them $40 for drinks when they finished and took off for the clubhouse. He hired two buckets of practice balls from the pro and went back to the hole where he made the wonder shot. Three hours and hundreds of balls later he scored another hole in one, and again the little man appeared. 'Ace Hole Leprechaun at your service, sir, and what would you wish this time?' Paddy replied, 'Could you make my legs a bit longer?'

At the fourteenth hole at Sherwood Park Golf Club in Whangarei the firm's toady was playing with the boss, who was the sort of player who couldn't hit a bull on the bum with a banjo. After the boss had hit three into the lake, the toady said, 'Gee, chief, you make a bigger splash with your shots than anyone else.'

When a couple got married, the wife put a very strong foot locker in the bedroom and put the key around her neck. 'That is my private foot locker,' she said, 'and until you die you will never know what's in there.' On their fiftieth wedding anniversary she relented and opened the box, and inside were two golf balls and $5,000 in cash. 'What're the golf balls for?' asked the husband, thinking she had taken some of his. 'Well,' she said, 'every time I've been unfaithful to you I charged your mates two golf balls.' That's not too bad, he thought, she has only been unfaithful to me once in 50 years. 'But where did the money come from?' he asked. 'That's from the sale of golf balls to the club professional.'

There was a foursome of ladies about to play a par three 145 yards long. Suddenly a streaker dashed out from the trees beside the fairway. One woman remarked, 'I think I know that guy. Isn't that Dick Green?' 'No,' replied another, 'I think it's a reflection off the grass.'

It was opening day at the golf club, a very good turnout it was too, and the course was extremely busy. On this particular day, a woman hit a badly misdirected shot that went through the trees and struck a gentleman on the next fairway. There was a cry of pain, and the woman dashed through the trees to find a man on the ground, in obvious pain, with his hands between his legs. She rushed over to him. 'Let me see,' she said. 'I am a trained nurse.' With that she lay the man down, undid his belt and started a soothing massage of his penis. 'How does that feel?' the woman asked her patient. 'Absolutely marvellous,' said the man, 'but my hand still hurts.'

MYTHS AND LEGENDS

This lawyer went out one morning and got into his car, but it wouldn't start. So he opened the bonnet and found that the battery was gone. In its place, however, was a note that read, 'I know this is unusual, but my battery went flat, and it was the middle of the night, and there was nothing I could do, so I took yours. I'm sorry for any inconvenience, but please find enclosed two tickets to the opera.' And indeed two opera tickets were enclosed. The lawyer was a bit annoyed by the loss of the battery, but he was glad of the opera tickets, and he and his wife duly went to the opera. They enjoyed it very much. But when they got home it was only to find that their house had been burgled in their absence.

This guy's walking on a beach in Thailand, and he looks down on the sand and he finds this 20-cent coin. He thinks, Ah, it could be my lucky day. So he goes up to this beachside café and there's a slot machine. He puts the 20 cents in it and he gets the jackpot, he gets $400. And he thinks, God, this is lucky. And a bit further down the beach is a casino, and he takes his $400 to the casino, and he goes to the blackjack table. He puts the $400 down and by the end of the evening he's won hundreds and hundreds of thousands of dollars. So he's sitting in the bar feeling really lucky and there's this woman there, this beautiful Indian woman, so beautiful. He's not really the kind of chap to ask women out, but he thinks, Today's my lucky day. So he says, 'Come out with me,' and she agrees. He can't believe his luck. They finally go to a

hotel and have a night of unbridled passion. In the morning he wakes up and he looks over and she's there still. So beautiful. On her forehead she's got a little red dot. He reaches over and scratches the dot and finds he's won a car.

On her way home from work this woman walked past the garage where her husband worked. She walked in and saw her husband's legs sticking out from under a car, so she bent down and ran her hand up his leg and fondled his balls. Poor guy! He was so surprised that he jerked up and banged his head on the bottom of the car and knocked himself out. Seeing the commotion a couple of the other guys there came over and saw what had happened and helped the woman drag the guy out. But he turned out not to be her husband, who was out test-driving a car. Finally, the ambulance came, and the mechanic, still unconscious, was loaded on to a stretcher. On the way to the ambulance, the ambulance attendants asked what had happened. When they heard, they started laughing, and they laughed so much that they tipped the guy off the stretcher, and he fell on the floor and broke his arm.

This chap goes travelling in Europe, and after a while he ends up in Copenhagen. Now, you know how they have that statue of a mermaid there? Well, this chap goes up to the mermaid and says, 'Have you ever been kissed?' She doesn't reply, so he leans towards her face and kisses her. 'Have you ever had your headlamps polished?' he says, and when there's no reply he leans towards her and fondles her breasts. Then he says, 'Have you ever been fucked?' Again there's no answer. And he says, 'Well you are now, the tide's gone out.'

This guy goes to a shrink and says, 'Doc, I'm real screwed up. Majorly. I think it's my name.' So the shrink asks, 'And what is your name?' The guy answers, 'Penis von Lesbian.' 'Oh,' says the shrink, 'indeed. I see your problem.' 'Yeah,' says the guy, 'so what am I going to do?' 'Easy,' said the shrink, 'change your name.' 'What to?' says the guy. 'How about Dick van Dyke?'

I FOUND IT IN MY E-MAIL

A man goes into his son's room to wish him goodnight. His son is having a nightmare. The man wakes him and asks him if he is okay. The son replies that he is scared because he dreamt that Aunt Susie had died. The father reassures the son that Aunt Susie is fine and tells him to go back to sleep. The next day, Aunt Susie dies. One week later, the man again goes into his son's room to wish him goodnight. His son is having another nightmare. The man again wakes his son. This time the son says that he dreamt that his grandfather died. The father assures him that his grandfather is fine and tells him to go back to sleep. The next day, the boy's grandfather dies. One week later, the man goes yet again into his son's room to wish him goodnight. And his son is having yet another nightmare. Again the man wakes his son. This time the son says that he had dreamt his Daddy had died. The father assures him that he is okay and tells the boy to go back to sleep. The man goes to bed but cannot sleep because he is so terrified. The next day, the man is scared for his life – he is sure he is going to die. After dressing and eating breakfast, he drives very carefully to work, fearful of a collision. He doesn't eat lunch because he is scared of food poisoning. He keeps his distance from everyone at his work, for he is sure that somehow he will be killed. He jumps at every noise, starts at every movement and ends up hiding under his desk . . . Upon walking in his front door at the end of the day, he sees his wife. 'Good God, dear,' he proclaims. 'I've just had the worst day of my entire life.' She responds,

'You think your day was bad. The milkman dropped dead on the doorstep this morning.'

A man walks into a chemist's and asks for a pack of condoms. As soon as he has paid for them, he starts laughing, and then walks out. The next day, the same performance, with the man walking out laughing fit to burst. The chemist thinks this is a bit odd and says to his assistant that if the man returns he is to follow him. Sure enough, the man comes into the shop the next day, repeating his routine once more. The assistant duly follows him when he leaves. Half an hour later, he returns. 'So did you follow him?' asks the chemist. 'I did,' says the assistant. 'And where did he go?' asks the chemist. The assistant replies, 'To your house.'

A boss had money problems and had to fire an employee, either Jack or Jill. He thought he'd fire whichever one came late to work the next morning. Well, both employees came to work very early. So he thought that he'd fire the first one who took a coffee break. Unfortunately for him, neither employee took a coffee break. Then the boss decided to see who took the longest lunch break, but strangely enough neither Jack nor Jill took a lunch break that day. They both ate at their desks. Then the boss thought he'd wait and see who left work the earliest, but both employees stayed after closing. Jill finally went to the coat rack and the boss went up to her and said, 'Jill, I have a terrible problem. I don't know whether to lay you or Jack off.' Jill said, 'Well, you'd better jack off, because I'm late for my bus.'

Why did the chicken cross the road?

Plato: For the greater good.

Karl Marx: To escape the bourgeois middle-class struggle.

Karl Marx (revisited): It was an historical inevitability.

Doug Hofstadter: To seek explication of the correspondence between appearance and essence through the mapping of the external road-object on to the internal road-concept.

Machiavelli: So that its subjects will view it with admiration, as a chicken which has the daring and courage to boldly cross the road, but also with fear, for whom among them has the strength to contend with such a paragon of avian virtue? In such a manner is the princely chicken's dominion maintained.

Hippocrates: Because of an excess of light pink gooey stuff in its pancreas.

Lovecraft: To futilely attempt escape from the dark powers which even then pursued it, hungering after the stuff of its soul.

Jacques Derrida: Any number of contending discourses may be discovered within the act of the chicken crossing the road, and each interpretation is equally valid as the authorial intent can never be discerned, because structuralism is DEAD, DAMMIT, DEAD!

Thomas de Torquemada: Give me 10 minutes with the chicken and I'll find out.

Robert Anton Wilson: Because agents of the Ancient Illuminated Roosters of Cooperia were controlling it with their Orbital Mind-Control Lasers as part of their master plan to take over the world's egg production.

Timothy Leary: Because that's the only kind of trip the Establishment would let it take.

Douglas Adams: Forty-two.

Friedrich Nietzsche: Because if you gaze too long across the Road, the Road gazes also across you.

Aleister Crowley: Because it was its True Will to do so.

Oliver North: National Security was at stake.

Sappho: For the touch of your skin, the sweetness of your lips . . .

J. R. R. Tolkein: Firstly, though, the chicken, sunlight coruscating off its radiant yellow-white coat of feathers, approached the dark, sullen asphalt road and scrutinised it intently with its obsidian-black eyes. Every detail of the thoroughfare leapt into blinding focus: the rough texture of the surface, over which countless tyres had worked their relentless tread through the ages; the innumerable fragments of stone embedded within the lugubrious mass, perhaps quarried from the great pits where the Sons of Man laboured not far from here; the dull black asphalt itself, exuding those waves of heat which distort the sight and bring weakness to the body; the other attributes of the great highway too numerous to give name. And then it crossed it.

Malcolm X: Because it would get across that road by any means necessary.

Skinner: Because the external influences which had pervaded its sensorium from birth had caused it to develop in such a fashion that it would tend to cross roads, even while believing these actions to be of its own free will.

Jung: The confluence of events in the cultural gestalt necessitated that individual chickens cross roads at this historical juncture, and therefore synchronicitously brought such occurrences into being.

Dorothy Parker: Travel, trouble, music, art
A kiss, a frock, a rhyme
But still they pass its time.

T. S. Eliot: It's not that they cross, but that they cross like chickens.

T. S. Eliot (again): Do I dare to cross the road?

Jean-Paul Sartre: In order to act in good faith and be true to itself, the chicken found it necessary to cross the road.

Jean-Luc Picard: To see what's out there.

Darth Vader: Because it could not resist the power of the Dark Side.

Ludwig Wittgenstein: The possibility of 'crossing' was encoded into the objects 'chicken' and 'road', and circumstances came into being which caused the actualisation of this potential occurrence.

Albert Einstein: Whether the chicken crossed the road or the road crossed the chicken depends upon your frame of reference.

Gandalf: O chicken, do not meddle in the affairs of roads, for you are tasty and good with barbecue sauce.

Aristotle: To actualise its potential.

Roseanne Barr: Urrrrrp. What chicken?

Julius Caesar: To come, to see, to conquer.

Candide: To cultivate its garden.

Buddha: If you ask this question, you deny your own chicken-nature.

Moses: Know ye that it is unclean to eat the chicken that has crossed the road, and that the chicken that crosseth the road doth so for its own preservation.

Joseph Conrad: Mistah Chicken, he dead.

Darwin: It was the logical next step after coming down from the trees.

Thomas de Quincy: Because it ran out of opium.

René Descartes: It had sufficient reason to believe it was dreaming anyway.

Emily Dickinson: Because it could not stop for death.

Bob Dylan: How many roads must one chicken cross?

Epicurus: For fun. It was forced to do so by the chicken-hole principle.

Ralph Waldo Emerson: It didn't cross the road; it transcended it.

Basil Fawlty: Oh, don't mind that chicken. It's from Barcelona.

Sigmund Freud: The chicken obviously was female and obviously interpreted the pole on which the crosswalk sign was mounted as a phallic symbol of which she was envious.

Robert Frost: To cross the road less travelled by.

Zsa Zsa Gabor: It probably crossed to get a better look at my legs, which, thank goodness, are very good, dahling.

Gilligan: The traffic started getting rough;
the chicken had to cross.
If not for the plumage of its peerless tail
the chicken would be lost,
the chicken would be lost!

Johann Friedrich von Goethe: The eternal hen-principle made it do it.

Ernest Hemingway: To die. In the rain.

Werner Heisenberg: We are not sure which side of the road the chicken was on, but it was moving very fast.

David Hume: Out of custom and habit.

Saddam Hussein: This was an unprovoked act of rebellion and we were quite justified in dropping 50 tons of nerve gas on it.

Lee Iacocca: It found a better car, which was on the other side of the road.

John Paul Jones: It has not yet begun to cross!

Martin Luther King: It had a dream.

James Tiberius Kirk: To boldly go where no chicken has gone before.

Stan Laurel: I'm sorry, Ollie. It escaped when I opened the run.

Leda: Are you sure it wasn't Zeus dressed up as a chicken? He's into that kind of thing, you know.

Gottfried von Leibniz: In this best possible world, the road was made for it to cross.

Groucho Marx: Chicken? What's all this talk about chicken? Why, I had an uncle who thought he was a chicken. My aunt almost divorced him, but we needed the eggs.

Gregor Mendel: To get various strains of roads.

John Milton: To justify the ways of God to men.

Sir Isaac Newton: 1 Chickens at rest tend to stay at rest. 2 Chickens in motion tend to cross the road.

Thomas Paine: Out of common sense.

Ronald Reagan: I forget.

Mr Scott: 'Cos ma wee transporter beam was na functioning properly. Ah canna work miracles, Captain!

William Shakespeare: I don't know why, but methinks I could rattle off a hundred-line soliloquy without much ado.

Sisyphus: Was it pushing a rock, too?

Socrates: To pick up some hemlock at the corner druggist.

The Sphinx: You tell me.

Mr T: If you saw me coming you'd cross the road too.

Margaret Thatcher: There was no alternative.

Dylan Thomas: To not go (*sic*) gentle into that good night.

Henry David Thoreau: To live deliberately . . . and suck all the marrow out of life.

Mark Twain: The news of its crossing has been greatly exaggerated.

George Washington: Actually it crossed the Delaware with me back in 1776. But most history books don't reveal that I bunked with a birdie during the duration.

⊙ ⊙ ⊙

Mae West: I invited it to come up and see me sometime.

Walt Whitman: To cluck the song of itself.

William Wordsworth: To have something to recollect in tranquillity.

Zeno of Elea: To prove it could never reach the other side.

Jack Nicholson: 'Cause it (*censored*) wanted to. That's the (*censored*) reason.

Pyrrho the Sceptic: What road?

Stephen Jay Gould: It is possible that there is a sociobiological explanation for it, but we have been deluged in recent years with sociobiological stories, despite the fact that we have little direct evidence about the genetics of behaviours and we do not know how to obtain it for the specific behaviours that figure most prominently in sociobiological speculation.

Joseph Stalin: I don't care. Catch it. I need its eggs to make my omelette.

A man and a woman are riding next to each other on a bus. The man sneezes, pulls out his wang and wipes the tip. The woman can't believe what she's just seen and decides that she is hallucinating. A few minutes pass. The man sneezes again. Again he pulls out his wang and wipes the tip. The woman is about to go nuts. She can't believe that such an outrageously misbehaved person exists. A few more minutes pass. The man sneezes yet again. And yet again he takes out his wang and wipes the tip. The woman has finally had enough. She turns to the man and says, 'Three times you've sneezed, and three times you've removed your penis from your pants to wipe it off! What the hell kind of degenerate are you?' The man replies, 'I'm sorry to have disturbed you, ma'am. I have a very rare condition such that when I sneeze, I have an orgasm.' The woman then says, 'What are you taking for it?' The man looks at her and says, 'Pepper.'

⊙ ⊙ ⊙

This little boy wakes up three nights in a row when he hears a thumping sound coming from his parents' room. Finally, one morning he goes to his mother and says, 'Mum, every night I hear you and Daddy making noises, and when I look in your room you're bouncing up and down on him.'

His mother is taken by surprise and says, 'Oh . . . well . . . ah . . . well, I'm bouncing on his stomach because he's fat and that makes him thin again.'

And the boy says, 'Well, it won't work!'

His mother says, 'Why?'

The boy replies, 'Because the lady next door comes by after you leave each day and blows him back up.'

A fellow stopped at a rural gas station and, after filling his tank, he paid the bill and bought himself a soft drink. He stood by his car to drink his cola while watching a couple of men working along the roadside. One man would dig a hole two or three feet deep and then move on. The other man came along behind and filled in the hole. Both men repeated this behaviour every 25 feet. The men worked right past the fellow with the soft drink, continuing down the road.

'I can't stand this,' said the man as he tossed the can into a trash container and headed down the road towards the men. 'Hold it . . . hold it!' he said to the men. 'Can you tell me what's going on here with this digging?' 'Well, we work for the City Council,' one of the men said. 'But one of you is digging a hole and the other fills it in. You're not accomplishing anything. Aren't you wasting the Council's money?'

'You don't understand, mister,' one of the men said, leaning on his shovel as he wiped his brow. 'Normally there's three of us . . . me, Rodney and Mike. I dig the hole, Rodney sticks in the tree and Mike here puts the dirt back. Now just 'cos Rodney's sick, that don't mean that Mike and me can't work.'

A woman accompanied her husband to the doctor's office. After the checkup the doctor took the wife aside and said,

'Your husband is suffering from severe long-term stress, and it is affecting his cardiovascular system. He's a good candidate for either a heart attack or a stroke. If you don't do the following four things, your husband will surely die. First, each morning, fix him a healthy breakfast and send him off to work in a good mood. Second, get him home at lunch time and make him a warm, nutritious meal and put him in a good frame of mind before he goes back to work. Third, for dinner, fix him an especially nice meal, and don't burden him with household chores. Fourth, and most important for invigorating him and relieving his stress, have sex with him several times a week and satisfy his every whim in bed.'

On the way home in the car, the husband turned to his wife and asked, 'I saw the doctor talking to you and he sure seemed serious. What did he tell you?'

His wife replied, 'He said you're going to die.'

As Mr Smith was on his death bed, he attempted to formulate a plan that would enable him to take at least some of his considerable wealth with him. He called for the three men he trusted most – his lawyer, his doctor and his minister. He told them, 'I'm going to give you each $30,000 in cash before I die. At my funeral, I want you to place the money in my coffin so that I can try to take it with me.' All three agreed to do this and were then given the money. At the funeral, each of them approached the coffin in turn and placed an envelope inside. Afterwards, while riding in the limousine to the cemetery, the minister said, 'I have to confess something to you fellows. Smith was a good churchman all his life, and I know he would have wanted me to do this. The church needed a new baptistery very badly, and I took $10,000 of the money he gave me and had one built. I only put $20,000 in the coffin.' The doctor then said, 'Well, since we're confiding in one another, I might as well tell you that I didn't put the full $30,000 in the coffin either. Smith had a disease that could have been diagnosed sooner if I'd had this new machine, but the machine cost $20,000 and I couldn't afford it then. I used $20,000 of the money to buy the machine so that I might be able to save another patient. I know that Smith would have wanted me to do that.' The lawyer then said, 'I'm ashamed of both of you. When I put my envelope into that coffin, it held my personal cheque for the full $30,000.'

A man woke up in a hospital bed and called for his doctor. He asked, 'Give it to me straight. How long have I got?' The doctor replied that he doubted that his patient would survive the night. The man then said, 'Call my lawyer.' When the lawyer arrived, the man asked for his doctor to stand on one side of the bed, while the lawyer was to stand on the other. The man then laid back and closed his eyes. When he remained silent for several minutes, the doctor asked what he had in mind. The man replied, 'Jesus died with a thief on either side, and I thought I'd check out the same way.'

A snake and a rabbit were racing along a pair of intersecting forest pathways one day when they collided at the point where the pathways met. They immediately began to argue with one another as to who was at fault for the mishap. When the snake remarked that he had been blind since birth, and thus should be given additional leeway, the rabbit said that he, too, had been blind since birth. The two animals then forgot about the collision and began commiserating concerning the problems of being blind. The snake said that his greatest regret was the loss of his identity. He had never been able to see his reflection in the water, and for that reason didn't know exactly what he looked like, or even what he really was. The rabbit declared that he had the same problem. Seeing a way that they could help each other, the rabbit proposed that they feel each other from head to toe, and then each try to describe the other. The snake agreed, and started things off by winding himself around the rabbit. After a few minutes, he announced, 'You've got very soft, fuzzy fur, long ears, big back feet and a little fuzzy ball for a tail. I think that you must be a rabbit.' The rabbit was much relieved to establish his identity, and then proceeded to return the favour to the snake. After feeling about the snake's body for a few minutes, he asserted, 'Well, you're scaly, you're slimy, you've got beady little eyes, you squirm and slither all the time and you've got a forked tongue. I think that you must be a lawyer.'

A mother and son were walking through a cemetery, and passed by a headstone inscribed, 'Here lies a good lawyer and an honest man.' The little boy read the headstone, looked up at his mother and asked, 'Mummy, why did they bury two men in the one grave?'

A lawyer was sitting in his office late one night, when Satan appeared before him. The Devil told the lawyer, 'I have a proposition for you. You can win every case you take on, for the rest of your life. Your clients will adore you, your colleagues will stand in awe of you and you will make embarrassing sums of money. All I want in exchange is your soul, your wife's soul, your children's souls, the souls of your parents, grandparents and parents-in-law, and the souls of all your friends and law partners.' The lawyer thought about this for a moment, then asked, 'So, what's the catch?'

A rather bad man died and met Satan in a room with three doors. Satan explained: 'I have good news and bad news. The bad news is that you have to spend eternity behind one of these doors. The good news is that you can take a peek behind each door before you make your choice.' So, the man opened the first door and saw a room full of people standing on their heads on a concrete floor. Not very nice, he thought. Opening the second door, he saw a room full of people standing on their heads on a wooden floor. Better, he thought, but best to check the last door. Upon opening the last door, he saw a room full of people standing waist-deep in excrement and sipping coffee. 'Of the three, this one looks best,' he said, and waded in to get something to drink while Satan closed the door. A few minutes later the door opened. Satan stuck his head in and said, 'Coffee break's over, back on your heads.'

After marrying a young filly, a 90-year-old geezer told his doctor that they were expecting a baby. 'Let me tell you a story,' said the doctor. 'An absent-minded fellow went hunting, but instead of a gun he picked up an umbrella. Suddenly a bear charged him. Pointing his umbrella at the bear, he shot and killed it on the spot.' 'Impossible!' the old geezer exclaimed. 'Somebody else must have shot the bear.' 'Exactly,' said the doctor.

A guy takes a parachute jump. He's falling, falling, falling. Then he pulls the cord. Nothing happens. Luckily, there is a second, emergency, cord, so he pulls that. Unluckily, nothing happens. So he's plummeting towards the ground. *Arrrhhhhhhhhhhhhhhhhhh*. And he's trying to work out how to fix this parachute when he sees another guy going up in a balloon. So, as they pass, he yells out, 'Do you know how to fix a parachute?' The other guy yells back, 'No, do you know how to fix a gas cooker?'

One night an American, an Englishman and a Scotsman walked into a pub. They all ordered a pint of beer. The American saw a fly in his beer. He fished it out and set the pint aside. The Englishman saw a fly in his beer also. He fished it out, but then continued drinking his beer. The Scotsman likewise saw a fly in his beer. He fished it out, picked it up by the wings, shook it above the glass and said, 'Come on – spit it out, that's my beer.'

I'm a trisexual. I'll try anything once.

I've got my shit together but I can't pick it up.

◎ ● ◎

A horse show is a bunch of horses showing their arses to a bunch of horses' arses who are showing their horses.

Why doesn't anyone fly Virgin Airlines?
Who'd want to fly on a plane that doesn't go all the way.

Chocolate is better than sex:

1 You can *get* chocolate.
2 'If you love me you'll swallow it' has real meaning with chocolate.
3 Chocolate satisfies even when it has gone soft.
4 You can safely have chocolate when you are driving.
5 You can make chocolate last as long as you want it to.
6 You can have chocolate even in front of your mother.
7 If you bite the nuts too hard the chocolate won't mind.
8 Two people of the same sex can have chocolate without being called nasty names.
9 The word 'commitment' doesn't scare off chocolate.
10 You can have chocolate on top of your desk during workhours without upsetting your co-workers.
11 You can ask a stranger for chocolate without getting your face slapped.
12 You don't get hairs in your mouth with chocolate.
13 With chocolate there's no need to fake it.
14 Chocolate doesn't make you pregnant.
15 You can have chocolate at any time of the month.
16 Good chocolate is easy to find.
17 You can have as many kinds of chocolate as you can handle.
18 You are never too young or too old for chocolate.
19 When you have great chocolate it doesn't keep your neighbours awake.
20 With chocolate, size doesn't matter. It's *all* good.

How can you tell that soap operas are fictional?
In real life, men aren't affectionate out of bed.

What should you give a man who has everything?
A woman to show him how to work it.

Why do black widow spiders kill their partners after mating?
To stop the snoring before it starts.

Why don't men have mid-life crises?
Because they stay stuck in adolescence.

How does a man show he's planning for the future?
He buys two cases of beer instead of one.

How was Colonel Sanders a typical male?
All he cared about were legs, breasts and thighs.

How is being at a singles bar different from going to the circus?
At the circus the clowns don't talk.

What makes men chase women they have no intention of marrying?
The same urge that makes dogs chase cars they have no intention of driving.

What do you do with a bachelor who thinks he's God's gift?
Exchange him.

Why do bachelors like smart women?
Opposites attract.

Why are husbands like lawnmowers?
They're hard to get started, emit foul odours and half the time they don't work.

What's the difference between a new husband and a new dog?
After a year the dog is still excited to see you.

Why is sleeping with a man like a soap opera?
Because just when it's getting interesting, they're finished until the next time.

Why do men find it difficult to make eye contact?
Because breasts don't have eyes.

What do men and beer bottles have in common?
They're both empty from the neck up.

How are men like noodles?
Because they're always in hot water, they lack taste and they need dough.

What do anniversaries and toilets have in common?
Men always miss them.

Why are men like popcorn?
Because they satisfy you, but only for a little while.

Why are men like blenders?
Because you need one, but you're not quite sure why.

Why is food better than men?
Because you don't have to wait an hour for seconds.

Why do so many women fake orgasm?
Because so many men fake foreplay.

Why are women so bad at mathematics?
Because men keep telling them that this [indicate a six-inch measure] is 12 inches.

Why do men like frozen microwave dinners so much?
Because they like being able to both eat and make love in under five minutes.

Why would women be better off if men treated them like cars?
Because at least then they would get a little attention every six months or 5,000 miles, whichever came first.

What do you call a man who expects to have sex on the second date?
Slow.

Why do men have a hole in the end of their penises?
So that oxygen can get to their brains.

What's the difference between men and pigs?
Pigs don't turn into men when they drink.

A girl phoned me the other day and said, 'Come on over, there's nobody home.' I went over. Nobody was home.

If it weren't for pickpockets I'd have no sex life at all.

I was born poor. Why, if I wasn't a boy I'd have nothing to play with.

During sex my girlfriend always wants to talk to me. Just the other night she called me from a hotel.

One day as I came home early from work I saw a guy jogging naked. I said to the guy, 'Hey, buddy, why are you jogging naked?' He said, 'Because you've come home early.'

It's been a rough day. I got up this morning, put on a shirt and a button fell off. I picked up my briefcase and the handle came off. I'm afraid to go to the bathroom.

I could tell that my parents hated me. My bath toys were a toaster and a radio.

My mother never breastfed me. She told me that she only liked me as a friend.

My father carries around the picture of the kid that came with his wallet.

When I was born the doctor came out to the waiting room and said to my father, 'I'm very sorry. We did everything we could, but he pulled through.'

My mother had morning sickness after I was born.

I remember the time I was kidnapped and they sent a piece of my finger to my father. He said he wanted more proof.

Once when I was lost I saw a policeman and asked him to help me find my parents. I said to him, 'Do you think we'll ever find them?' He said, 'I don't know, kid. There's so many places they can hide.'

On Halloween the parents used to send their kids out looking like me. One year one kid tried to rip my face off. Now I'm a grown-up it's different. When I answer the door the kids give me candy.

My wife made me join a bridge club. I jump off next Tuesday.

I worked in a pet shop, and people kept asking how big I'd get.

I went to see my doctor. 'Doctor,' I said, 'every morning when I get up and look in the mirror I feel like throwing up. What's wrong with me?' He said, 'I don't know, but your eyesight is perfect.'

OUT ON THE NET

Willie saw some dynamite,
Didn't understand it quite.
Curiosity never pays,
It rained Willie seven days.

What's the difference between a blonde and a light bulb?
The light bulb is smarter, but the blonde is easier to turn on.

How can you tell when a fax has been sent by a blonde?
There is a stamp on it.

What does a blonde say when you ask her if her blinker is on?
'It's on, it's off, it's on . . .'

What do you call a basement full of blondes?
A wine cellar.

What do you call a blonde between two brunettes?
A mental block.

What happened when the blonde and brunette jumped off a 20-storey building?
The brunette hit the pavement, but not the blonde – she got lost.

What do you do when a blonde throws a pin at you?
Run. She's got a hand-grenade in her mouth.

How do you drown a blonde?
Put a mirror at the bottom of her swimming pool.

Why do blondes hate M&Ms?
Because they're too hard to peel.

Why couldn't the blonde write the number 11?
Because she didn't know which 1 came first.

Why do blondes have more fun?
Because they are easier to keep amused.

Why won't a blonde eat pickles?
Because she can't get her head in the jar.

Why were blondes created?
Because sheep can't bring beer from the fridge.
Why were brunettes created?
Because neither could the blondes.

Did you hear about the blonde who shot an arrow into the air?
She missed.

Why can't blondes count to 70?
Because 69 is a bit of a mouthful.

What's the mating call of a blonde?
'I'm so drunk!'
What's the mating call of a brunette?
'When is that blonde bitch going to leave?'
What's the mating call of a redhead?
'Next!'

How does a blonde commit suicide?
She gathers her clothes into a pile and jumps off.

Why do blondes wear green lipstick?
Because red means stop.

Do you know why the blonde got fired from the M&M factory?
For throwing out the W's.

What's brown and red and black and blue?
A brunette who's told one too many blonde jokes.

How many blondes does it take to screw in a light bulb?
Blondes screw in back seats, not in light bulbs, silly.

Why don't blondes double recipes?
The oven doesn't go to 700 degrees.

Why don't blondes breast feed?
Because it hurts too much when they boil their nipples.

What do you call a blonde with two brain cells?
Pregnant.

What does a blonde owl say?
'What, what?'

Did you hear about the blonde lesbian?
She kept having affairs with men.

What does a blonde do if she is not in bed by 10?
She picks up her purse and goes home.

Why won't they hire blonde pharmacists?
They keep breaking the prescription bottles in the typewriter.

What's a blonde's idea of safe sex?
Locking the car door.

A blonde died and went to heaven. When she got to the Pearly Gates, she met Saint Peter, who said, 'Before you get to come into heaven, you have to pass a test.'

'Oh, no!' she said, but Saint Peter said not to worry, he'd make it easy.

'Who was God's son?' said Saint Peter.

The blonde thought for a few minutes and then said, 'Andy!'

'That's interesting . . . What made you say that?' said Saint Peter.

Then the blonde started to sing, 'Andy walks with me. Andy talks with me. Andy tells me . . .'

Two blondes were observed in a parking lot trying to unlock the door of their Mercedes with a coat hanger.

Blonde number 1: 'I can't seem to get this door unlocked.'

Blonde number 2: 'Well, you'd better hurry up. It's starting to rain and the top is down.'

Did you hear about the blonde who stayed up all night to see where the sun went?
It finally dawned on her.

A blonde was driving down the highway to Disneyland when she saw a sign that said DISNEYLAND LEFT. After thinking for a minute, she said to herself, 'Oh, well,' and turned around and drove home.

Did you hear about the suicide blonde?
She dyed by her own hand.

A policeman pulled a blonde over because she'd been driving the wrong way down a one-way street.

Cop: 'Do you know where you were going?'

Blonde: 'No, but wherever it is, it must be bad because all the people there were leaving.'

There were three women stranded on an island, a brunette, a redhead and a blonde. The brunette looked over the water to the mainland and estimated that it was about 20 miles to shore. So she announced, 'I'm going to try to swim to shore.' So she swam out five miles, and got really tired. And when she'd swam out 10 miles she was too tired to go on, so she drowned.

The second one, the redhead, said to herself, 'I wonder if she made it? Whatever . . . I guess it's better to try to get to the mainland than stay here and starve.' So she attempted to swim out. The redhead had a lot more endurance than the brunette, as she swam out 10 miles before she even got tired. After 15 miles, though, she was too tired to go on, so she drowned.

So the blonde thought to herself, 'I wonder if they made it? I think I'd better try to make it, too.' So she swam out five miles, 10 miles, 15 miles, 19 miles from the island. Finally, the further shore was just in sight, but she said, 'I'm too tired to go on!' Then she swam back.

A blonde and a brunette were talking one day. The brunette said that her boyfriend had a slight dandruff problem but she gave him Head and Shoulders and it cleared it up. The blonde asked inquisitively, 'How do you give shoulders?'

A blonde was bragging about her knowledge of the state capitals. She proudly said, 'Go ahead, ask me, I know all of them.'

A redhead said, 'Okay, what's the capital of Wisconsin?'

The blonde replied, 'Oh, that's easy. W.'

Why do blondes drive cars with sunroofs?
More leg room.

How do you tell when a blonde reaches orgasm?
She drops her nail-file.

How many blondes does it take to change a light bulb?
1 'What's a light bulb?'
2 One. She holds the bulb and the world revolves around her.
3 Two. One to hold the Diet Pepsi, and one to call, 'Daddy!'

How do you get a one-armed blonde out of a tree?
Wave at her.

Why did the blonde scale the glass wall?
To see what was on the other side.

How many blondes does it take to make chocolate chip cookies?
Three. One to mix the batter and two to squeeze the rabbit.

There's three blondes sitting on a couch. How do you know which one is the cocksucker?
The one spitting feathers.

Why does a blonde eat beans on Saturday?
So she can take a bubble bath on Sunday.

How many blondes does it take to screw in a light bulb?
A hundred. One to screw it in and 99 to say, 'I can do that.'

Why didn't the blonde get the elevator job?
Because she didn't know the route.

How can you tell if a blonde's been using the computer?
There's white-out on the screen.
How can you tell if another blonde's been using the computer?
There's writing on the white-out.

How can you tell if a blonde has been in your refrigerator?
Because there's lipstick on your cucumbers.

Why did the blonde keep a coat hanger in her back seat?
In case she locked the keys in the car.

On her way home, the blonde drove past a sign that said CLEAN RESTROOMS 8 MILES. By the time she'd driven the eight miles, she had cleaned 43 restrooms.

Did you hear about the blonde who sniffed Equal?
She thought it was Diet Coke.

What did the blonde do when she saw the commercial that said '90% of all accidents occur within a two-mile radius of your home'?
She moved.

Why did the blonde stop using the pill?
Because it kept falling out.

o o o

On their first date, Joe took Rose to the carnival. When he asked her what she wanted to do first, Rose replied, 'Get weighed.'

So Joe took her to the man with the scales who guesses your weight. He looked at Rose and said, 'One hundred and twenty pounds.' Since Rose weighed in at one seventeen, she collected a prize.

Next they went on the roller coaster. When the ride was finished, Joe asked Rose what she wanted to do next. 'Get weighed,' she said. So they went back to the man with the scales, who of course guessed Rose's weight correctly. Leaving without a prize, they went for a ride on the merry-go-round. After they got off, Joe asked Rose what she wanted to do next. 'I want to get weighed,' she said again.

Now Joe began to think this girl was quite strange, and decided to end the evening quickly. He left her at her door with a quick handshake. Rose's roommate was waiting up for her return and asked how the evening went. 'Wousy!' Rose replied.

Adam was taking a walk in the Garden of Eden, having his daily chat to God. The following conversation took place.

Adam: 'Thank you so much for giving Eve to me. She's made such a difference in my life. I just have one question: Why did you have to make her so beautiful? I can't keep my eyes and my hands off her.'

God: 'Well, Adam, I had to make her so beautiful so you could love her.'

Satisfied with this Adam went off to find Eve.

The following day he was involved in another conversation with God.

o o o

Adam: 'God, I understand that you had to make Eve beautiful so I could love her, but I don't understand why you had to make her so stupid.'

God: 'Well, Adam, I had to make her so stupid so she could love you.'

Justice of the Peace (to a bride who teaches linguistics): 'Do you take this man to be your lawful wedded husband, in good times or in bad?'

Bride (after brief pause): 'In good times.'

I asked my wife if she would ever get married again if I died. She said, 'Yeah, I'm still young so I probably would.' I asked her if she would let him drive my car. She said, 'Yeah, it's a nice car so I'd let him drive it.' I asked her if she would let him sleep in our bed. She said, 'Yeah, it's nice and comfortable so I would let him sleep in it.' Then I asked her if she would let him use my golf clubs and she replied, 'No, he's left-handed.'

Why do men want to marry virgins?
They can't stand criticism.

What are two reasons why men don't mind their own business?
1 No mind.
2 No business.

Why do men like masturbation?
Because it's sex with someone they love.

What is a man's view of safe sex?
A padded headboard.

o o o

An Irishman was stopped at Customs after returning from a holiday on the Continent.

'What's in this bottle?' asked the customs officer, taking out a large bottle from the Irishman's suitcase.

'Oh,' said the Irishman, 'that is only Holy Water from Lourdes.'

'Hmm!' muttered the customs officer as he took the top off the bottle and sniffed the liquid inside. Then he tasted some of it. 'It looks, smells and tastes very much like whisky to me, sir.'

'Glory be,' replied the Irishman, ''tis another miracle!'

An Irishman driving down the road got pulled over by a policeman. The policeman, observing him, said, 'You're drunk.' The driver said, 'Thank God for that, I thought the steering had gone.'

God made whisky to prevent the Irish from taking over.

An Irishman wanted to join an amateur baseball team. The coach looked him over and decided to give him a chance.

'I will ask you three questions,' said the coach. 'If you come back in a week and answer them all correctly, you're on the team.'

'Fair enough,' said the Irishman eagerly.

The coach proceeded, 'Here are your questions. First, how many days are there in a week that start with the letter t? Second, how many seconds are there in a year? And third, how many d's are there in "Rudolph the Red-Nosed Reindeer"?'

Next week, the Irishman returned, feeling confident that he knew the right answers. The coach said, 'So, how many days are there in the week that start with t?'

The Irishman said, 'Two.'

'Very good,' said the coach. 'And what are they?'

'Today and tomorrow.'

'Hmm . . . Okay,' said the coach. 'How many seconds are there in a year?'

'Twelve.'

'Twelve? How did you come up with twelve?' The coach was perplexed.

'Well,' said the Irishman, 'there's the second of January, the second of February, the second of . . .'

'Umm . . . Okay,' broke in the coach. 'Now, how many d's in "Rudolph the Red-Nosed Reindeer"?'

'Oh, that's easy,' laughed the Irishman. 'Three hundred and sixty-five.'

'*What?*' cried the coach. 'How did you get that figure?'

To which the Irishman replied, 'Dee dee dee-dee-dee dee-dee . . .'

An Irishman saw a priest walking down the street. Noticing his collar, he stopped him and said, 'Excuse me, but why are you wearing your shirt backwards?'

The priest laughed, 'Because, my son, I am a Father.'

The Irishman scratched his head. 'But I am a father too, and I don't wear my shirt backwards!'

Again the priest laughed. 'But I am a father of thousands.'

To which the Irishman replied, 'Well, then you should wear your underwear backwards.'

An Irishman went to a carpenter and said, 'Can you build me a box that is two inches high, two inches wide and fifty feet long?'

'Hmm . . .' mused the carpenter. 'It could be done, I suppose, but what do you want it for?'

'Well, you see,' said the Irishman, 'my neighbour moved away and forgot his garden hose, so I was going to send it to him.'

An Irishman wanted to learn how to sky dive. He got an instructor and started lessons. The instructor told the Irishman to jump out of the plane and pull his rip cord. The instructor then explained that he himself would jump out right behind him so that they would go down together. The Irishman understood and was ready.

The time came for the Irishman to jump from the airplane. The instructor reminded the Irishman that he would be right behind him. The Irishman proceeded to jump from the plane, and after being in the air for a few seconds pulled the rip cord. The instructor followed and jumped from the plane. The instructor pulled his rip cord but the parachute did not open. The instructor, frantically trying to get his parachute open, plummeted past the Irishman.

The Irishman, seeing this, yelled, as he undid the straps to his parachute, 'So you wanna race, eh?'

These two Irishmen are building a house. One of them is putting on the siding. He picks up a nail and hammers it in. He picks up another nail, but throws it away. He picks up a nail, hammers it in. Picks up another, throws it away. This goes on for a while, and finally his friend comes over and asks him why he is throwing half of the nails away.

The Irishman replies, 'Those ones were pointed on the wrong end.'

The buddy gets exasperated and says, 'You idiot, those are for the other side of the house.'

An Irishman was jumped by two muggers and fought like hell, but was finally subdued. His attackers then proceeded to go through his pockets. 'You mean you fought like that for 57 cents?' asked one of the muggers incredulously.

'Is that all you wanted?' moaned the Irishman. 'I thought you were after the $400 in my shoe.'

An Irishman is hired to paint the lines on the road. On the first day he painted 10 miles, and his employers were amazed. But on the second day he painted just five, and, on the third day, he painted only a mile of the road. Disappointed, his boss asked him what the problem was. The Irishman replied, 'Well, sir, every day I have to walk farther and farther to get back to the bucket of paint.'

You go to a cockfight. How do you know if there's an Irishman there?
He's the one with a duck.
How do you know if an Italian is there?
He's the one who bet on the duck.
How do you know if the Mafia is there?
The duck wins.

The newly opened shopping centre had three tailors – all with shops next to each other. As another coincidence, all three tailors were named Jacob Silverstein.

The first tailor put up a sign over his shop which proclaimed: 'Jacob Silverstein – High Class Tailor.'

The second tailor put up a sign saying: 'Silverstein – The Tailor of Distinction.'

The third tailor's sign was smaller and it said: 'Silverstein's Tailors – Main Entrance.'

A Jewish man walks into a bar and sits down. He has a few drinks, then he sees a Chinese man and walks over and punches him in the face. 'Ouch!' the Chinese man says. 'What was that for?' 'That was for Pearl Harbour,' the Jewish man says. 'But I'm Chinese!' 'Chinese, Japanese, what's the difference?' And the Jewish man sits back down. Then, the Chinese man walks up to the Jewish man and punches him in the face. 'Ouch!' the Jewish man says. 'What was that for?' 'That was for the *Titanic*,' the Chinese man says. 'But that was an iceberg!' 'Iceberg, Goldberg, what's the difference?'

An American general and a Russian general are discussing troop rations. The Russian says, 'Every day, each soldier consumes 1500 calories.' 'Oh, yeah?' says the American. 'Well our troops consume 3000 calories a day.' 'This is not possible,' replies the Russian. 'How can one man eat an entire sack of potatoes?'

These two Polish guys rent a boat and go fishing at a lake. They are amazed at the number of fish they catch that day, and one says to the other, 'We'll have to come back here tomorrow!'

The other asks, 'But how will we remember where this spot is?'

The first guy then takes a can of spray paint, paints an X on the bottom of the boat, and says, 'We'll just look for this X tomorrow.'

The other guy says, 'You idiot! How do you know we'll get the same boat?'

Two Polish truck drivers are barrelling along when they come to an overpass. A sign says, 'Clearance: 11' 2".' They get out, measure their truck, and realise that it's 11' 6". So the first Pole looks at the second Pole and says, 'I don't see any cops around . . . let's go for it!'

A guy walks into a bar, sits downs and starts to make conversation with the guy at the next table. 'Want to hear the world's worst Polish joke?' he says.

The second guy says, 'Sure, but before you tell it, let me tell you something. See those two bikers over there by the door, those real mean motherfuckers? They're Polish. And those two bouncers by the bar? They're Polish too. The bartender? Polish. And one more thing, pal, I'm Polish too. Now, still want to tell that joke?'

'Hell, no,' replies the first guy, 'I don't want to have to explain it six times.'

Two Polish hunters were out looking for pheasant when they came upon the local farmer's daughter, sitting naked on a fence, sunning herself.

The first hunter asked, 'Are you game?'

She replied, 'I sure am, honey!'

The second hunter shot her.

Two Poles are flying across Europe in a 727, a three-engined plane, when the pilot announces, 'Folks, we just had one engine go out but, don't worry, this plane can fly just fine on two engines. However, we're going to be about an hour late getting into Warsaw.'

An hour later, the pilot gets on the intercom again. 'Folks, don't get alarmed, but a second engine just went. Please don't worry, though – this plane is designed to fly safely on one engine; but now we'll be about two hours late getting into Warsaw.'

After that announcement, one Pole looks at the other and says, 'Well, I sure hope that third engine doesn't go. We'll be up here all night.'

Stalin is dying, and he summons Comrade Khrushchev to his bedside. Wheezing his last few words with difficulty, Stalin tells Khrushchev, 'Comrade, the reins of the country are now in your hands. But before I go, I want to give you some advice.'

'Yes, yes, Great Leader, what is it?' says Khrushchev.

Reaching under his pillow, Stalin produces two envelopes, marked 1 and 2. 'Take these letters,' he tells Khrushchev. 'Keep them safely – don't open them. However, if it should happen that the country is in turmoil and things start going badly, then open the first one. That'll give you some advice on what to do. And, even after that, if things start going *really* badly, open the second one.' And with a gasp Stalin breathed his last.

Well, Khrushchev succeeded him, and, sure enough, within a few years things started going badly – unemployment increased, crops failed, people became restless. Nikita decided it was time to open the first letter. All it said was: 'Blame everything on me!' So Khrushchev launched a massive de-Stalinisation campaign, and blamed Josef for all the excesses and purges and ills of the present system, and bought himself some time that way.

But things continued on the downslide – Kennedy successfully rebuffed Soviet missiles in Cuba, unemployment increased, crops failed, the Politburo was unhappy with Khrushchev's leadership and upstarts like Brezhnev and Gromyko were threatening his credibility. So finally, after much deliberation, Nikita opened the second letter.

All it said was: 'Write two letters.'

A compulsive gambler at the roulette table was having a particularly bad run of luck when suddenly he heard a soft, ghostly voice in his ear say, 'Number seven.'

The gambler furtively looked behind him, but there was no one near him who could possibly have made such a ghostly whisper. However, he decided he had nothing to lose by backing the advice of the mysterious whisperer.

The number came up – number seven, and it won the gambler a small sum of money, but not enough to cover his earlier losses, so the gambler continued at the table. Again, the ghostly voice whispered, 'Number seven,' and the gambler followed the advice and won yet again.

This went on for some considerable time. Just before the gambler placed each bet the ghostly voice would whisper, 'Number seven,' and the number seven always came up.

After this had happened nine times in succession, the gambler had collected quite a number of interested spectators – as well as winning well over $10,000.

Then the ghostly voice whispered, 'Put everything on number five.' The gambler was surprised at the change in directions, but he decided to continue to follow the advice given him by the strange ghostly voice.

The roulette wheel spun round, the gambler held his breath, the crowd round the table watched with astonishment – and the ball landed in number seven. And the ghostly voice in the gambler's ears said, 'Damn!'

Before going to Europe on business, a man drove his Rolls-Royce to a downtown New York City bank and went in to ask for an immediate loan of $5,000. The loan officer, taken aback, requested collateral. 'Well, then, here are the keys to my Rolls-Royce,' the man said. The loan officer promptly had the car driven into the bank's underground parking for safe keeping, and gave the man $5,000.

Two weeks later, the man walked through the bank's doors, and asked to settle up his loan and get his car back. 'That will be $5,000 in principal, and $15.40 in interest,' the loan officer said. The man wrote out a cheque and started to walk away.

'Wait, sir,' the loan officer said, 'while you were gone, I found out you are a millionaire. Why in the world would you need to borrow $5,000?'

The man smiled. 'Where else could I park my Rolls-Royce in Manhattan for two weeks and pay only $15.40?'

Courtier: 'Sire, the people are revolting!'
King: 'Yes, very.'

What do you get when you cross an insomniac, a dyslexic and an agnostic?
Someone who sits up all night wondering if there really is a Dog.

Concerning Chinese tobacco: Many men smoke, but Fu Manchu.

He who can can can can cans of corn.

'It's not just the work I enjoy,' said the taxi driver. 'It's the people I run into.'

Did you hear about the ship that ran aground carrying a cargo of red and black paint?
The whole crew was marooned.

What was wrong with the wooden car?
It wooden go.

If you've heard one cliché, you've heard 'em all.

How far can a person walk into a forest?
Only halfway, because after that he would be walking out of the forest.

If a tree falls in the forest with no one to hear it, who will notify the next of kindling?

Computer: the only productivity tool that costs as much time and money as it saves.

Did you hear about the two corpuscles who fell in love in vein?

Be naughty. Save Santa a trip!

How much dirt can you get out of a four-cubic-foot hole?
None. It's a hole.

Politicians are like a bunch of bananas. They start off green, turn yellow and there isn't a straight one in the bunch.

First cannibal: 'I don't think much of your wife.'
Second cannibal: 'Just eat the chips then.'

Did you hear about the midget on the crowded subway?
He had his nose in everybody's business.

⊙ ⊙ ⊙

What's the difference between a dressmaker and an alto?
The dressmaker tucks up the frills . . .

Why do bagpipers walk when they play?
To get away from the noise.

What is the definition of alto?
A low form of singing indulged in by some women.

⊙ ⊙ ⊙

What's brown and sounds like a bell?
Dung!

What's white and fluffy and swings through the cake shop?
A meringue-utang.

'That's my favourite song,' Tom said off the record.

'I love mathematics,' Tom added.

'Look, it's Free Willy,' Tom wailed out.

'I dropped my toothpaste,' Tom said crestfallen.

'I just got a pacemaker,' Tom said half-heartedly.

'I'm not sure if I'm a homosexual,' said Tom, half in Ernest.

'I couldn't perform!' Tom said limply.

What do you get when you cross the Godfather with a lawyer?
An offer you can't understand.

What do you get when you cross Lee Iacocca with Count Dracula?
autoexec.bat

What do bees do with honey?
They cell it.

How can you fix a broken tomato?
With tomato paste.

A psychiatrist is treating a group of delusional patients. These patients are confused about who they are, some believing they are famous people from history. The doctor is sure he can help them if he can just get them to think logically, so he calls them to his office. The first patient is a man named Smith, who thinks that he's Napoleon. 'How are you, Mr Smith?' asks the doctor. 'I'm not this "Smith", I am Napoleon Bonaparte,' comes the indignant reply. 'Well, how do you know you're Napoleon?' asks the doctor, carefully trying to get Mr Smith to examine his thinking. The man stuffs his hand in his shirt front and says, 'Because God made me Napoleon.' A smug little grin begins to creep across his face, as if he's won the argument, when, suddenly, the squeaky, high-pitched voice of another patient rings out, 'No I didn't.'

The tea manufacturers wanted a new advertising gimmick, so the senior creative man at their advertising agency decided to go to Rome to see if he could persuade the Pope to make a TV commercial.

The Pope gave the adman an audience and he made his request. 'We'll give you £1,000 for a 10-second commercial. All you have to do is say, "Give us this day our daily tea."'

'I'm sorry,' replied the Pope, 'but I cannot do as you request.'

'Five hundred thousand,' offered the adman.

'I'm afraid not,' said the Pope, solemnly.

'All right. One million pounds. And that's our very last offer.'

But still the Pope refused to make the commercial, and the adman left. On the way home the adman turned to his secretary and said, 'That's odd. I mean, the Pope refusing to do a commercial for tea. I wonder how much the bread people are giving him.'

A man rushed into a pub in a rather agitated state. 'Does anyone here own a large black cat with a white collar?' he asked, somewhat nervously. There was no reply.

'Does anybody own a large black cat with a white collar?' asked the man again, raising his voice even higher above the general noise of the bar. But still no one answered his question.

'Oh, dear,' muttered the man. 'I must have run over the vicar.'

Do you know what happens when a short-legged cow tries to jump a fence?
It's an udder disaster.

What's the last thing to go through a bug's mind as it hits the windshield?
Its arse.

What do you get when you cross an elephant with peanut butter?
Peanut butter with a good memory.
or
An elephant that sticks to the roof of your mouth.

If a rooster sitting on the ridge of a roof lays an egg, which way will it fall?
Neither way. Roosters don't lay eggs.

An 85-year-old man got married to a 35-year-old woman. The old man was playing draughts down at the senior citizens centre when his opponent congratulated him on his recent marriage. After several draught moves he said, 'I'll bet she is nice-looking.' 'No,' said the old man. 'She is rather ordinary in appearance.' Several minutes later the other man said,

'Well, I'll bet she is a good cook.' 'Well, no,' replied the newlywed. 'In fact, we eat all of our meals at various restaurants.'

Several more minutes passed as the draughts game continued. 'Well, I'll bet she has lots of money.' 'No,' said the old man, 'in fact, she was completely broke when we met.' Exasperated, the other man asked, 'Well, why in the world did you marry her?' The old man said, 'I needed someone who could drive at night.'

Fred and his wife, Thelma, were going to a big Halloween party. At the last minute, Thelma said she felt sick and told Fred to go to the party without her. He did. Shortly after he left, Thelma started to feel better. So she put on a sheet and went to the party dressed as a ghost. When she arrived, she was shocked and hurt to discover Fred dancing and flirting with every girl in the place. She devised a scheme: she would go over and try to seduce Fred (still in her costume) and see how faithful he was. 'Hey, big boy,' she said to Fred, 'want to see what's under my sheet?' That was all it took. The two went outside together and had wild sex on the lawn. Before she could be unmasked and her identity exposed, Thelma ran home and went to bed. Hours later, Fred walked in. 'So, dear,' said Thelma in a heavy, sarcastic tone, 'How was the *party?*' Fred hedged and stammered. 'Well, uh, you know . . . it was all right.' Thelma pressed further: 'Did you meet anyone interesting at the party?' 'Well, er, um . . . no, not really.' Sure that she had him, Thelma moved in for the kill: 'What was the most exciting part of the party?' Fred squirmed a little more and finally gave a straight answer. 'Actually, when I arrived there without you I was pretty bored and I went out back with George and Eddie to play cards. But wait'll you hear what happened to the guy I lent my costume to.'

There are three mental patients being considered for release, so this professor comes to ask them all a question. The first patient comes in and the professor says, 'What is two and two?' The first patient says, 'five thousand,' and the professor says, 'I'm sorry, that's not correct.'

The second patient comes in and the professor asks the patient, 'What is two and two?', and the patient says, 'Tuesday.' The professor says, 'Sorry, you're wrong.' The third patient comes in and the professor asks the same question. This time the patient says, 'Four.' The professor is amazed and asks how he got the answer. To that the patient replies, 'I divided 5,000 by Tuesday.'

There once was a man from Racine,
Who invented a loving machine.
Both concave and convex, it could serve either sex,
And it serviced itself in between.

The Scottish town of Fife, a well-known fishing centre, hosts an annual international competition whose winner is the one who manages to consume the greatest quantity of fish. The particular variety of fish involved is tench, a local favourite, abundant off the North Sea coast and exported throughout the whole EEC. Last year, a local man by the name of Hicks was by many favoured to win this gastronomic contest, while others predicted the victory of a former champion from Finland, Sven Oorslaatd. Hicks was a simple fisherman who had long neglected the dental work he required, and in the fiery passion of the final stages of the competition he was bitterly frustrated by the dislodging of one of his bottom molars while completing his eighth portion, causing his loss.

The ensuing victory for the Finn was announced by the local papers the next morning in the following headline: ONE TOOTH FREE FOR FIFE'S HICKS: SVEN ATE NINE TENCH.

A distinguished linguistics professor was lecturing on the phenomenon of double negatives. As he neared the end of his talk, he drew himself up and declared solemnly: 'In conclusion, let me observe that while there are numerous cases where a double negative conveys a positive, there is no case where a double positive conveys a negative.' Whereupon, from the back of the room, arose a small voice dripping with disdainful condescension: 'Yeah, yeah . . .'

A bounty hunter went into a bar in Mexico to look for a man who had been robbing banks in Texas. He found the man and put a gun up to his head and said, 'Where's the money?' Another man came up and said, 'Him don't know English. I will interpret for you.' The bounty hunter said, 'Okay, tell him that I will blow his head off if he doesn't tell me where the money is.' So this man talked to the other man who told him to go to the brick building on the corner and count three bricks up and three bricks to the right and there he would find the money. The bounty hunter asked, 'What did he say?' The man said, 'Oh, senor. He said he don't care. Blow his head off.'

We all know Santa as a fat, jolly old man. Well, he may be fat and he may be old, but he ain't always jolly. There was this one year when Mrs Claus decided she wanted to be a feminist, the reindeer went on strike and the elves sued because they wanted to be called 'vertically challenged toy manufacturers' instead of elves. Santa had just retreated to his office to rest when an angel entered and said, 'Santa . . .' 'What do you want?' was the reply. 'Well,' the angel answered, 'the Christmas tree arrived today.' 'So?' Santa said. 'Well, I was wondering where you wanted me to put it.' . . . And that, my friends, is why angels sit on top of Christmas trees.

A little boy came home from school one day and said to his father, 'Dad, what can you tell me about politics? I have to learn about it for school tomorrow.' The father thought some and said, 'Okay, son, the best way I can describe politics is to use an analogy. Let's say that I'm capitalism because I'm the breadwinner. Your mother will be government because she controls everything, our maid will be the working class because she works for us, you will be the people because you answer to us, and your baby brother will be the future. Does that help any?' The little boy said, 'Well, Dad, I don't know, but I'll think about what you said.'

Later that night, after everyone had gone to bed, the little boy was woken up by his brother's crying. Upon further investigation, he found a dirty nappy. So, he went down the hall to his parents' bedroom and found his father's side of the bed empty and his mother fast asleep. Then he saw a light on in the guest room down the hall, and, when he reached the door, he saw through the crack that his father was in bed with the maid. Because he couldn't do anything else, he returned to his bedroom and went back to bed.

The next morning, he said to his father at the breakfast table, 'Dad, I think I understand politics much better now.' 'Excellent, my boy,' his father answered. 'What have you learned?' The little boy thought for a minute and said, 'I learned that capitalism is screwing the working class, government is sound asleep ignoring the people, and the future's full of shit.'

OUT ON THE NET AGAIN

How many drummers does it take to change a light bulb?
None. They have machines to do that now.

How many Australians does it take to change a light bulb?
Sixteen. One to change the bulb and 15 to stand around saying, 'Goodonya mate.'

How many Australians does it take to change a light bulb?
One, but you have to pry him off the sheep first.

How many surrealists does it take to change a light bulb?
Three. One to screw in the bulb, one to hold the giraffe and one to fill the bathtub with brightly coloured power-tools.

How many Marxist-Leninists does it take to screw in a light bulb?
None. The light bulb contains the seeds of its own revolution.

How many possums does it take to change a light bulb?
Two. One to change it and the other to watch out for traffic.

How many divorced men does it take to change a light bulb?
None. The sockets all went with the house.

How many liberated women does it take to change a light bulb?
Five. One to turn the bulb and four to form a support group.

How many politicians does it take to change a light bulb?
Four. One to change it and the other three to deny that it's been changed.

How many MPs does it take to change a light bulb?
Twenty-one. One to change it and 20 to form a fact-finding committee to learn more about how it was done.

How many Thatcherites does it take to change a light bulb?
None. It's up to the private sector to provide the finance for it.

How many economists does it take to change a light bulb?
None. If the light bulb really needed changing, market forces would have already caused it to happen.

How many Liberals does it take to change a light bulb?
One Liberal and 28 delegates representing all the social, economic and ethnic communities.

How many social scientists does it take to change a light bulb?
Social scientists do not change light bulbs. They search for the root cause as to why the last one went out.

How many Conservatives does it take to change a light bulb?
One; after reflecting in the twilight on the merit of the previous bulb.

How many Socialists does it take to change a light bulb?
One thousand and fifty-one. One to petition the Ministry of Light for a bulb, 50 to establish the state production quota, 200 militia to force the factory unions to allow production of

the bulb, and one to surreptitiously dial an 0800 number to order an American light bulb.

How many Libertarians does it take to change a light bulb?
None. If the libertarian wants to sit in the dark, it's his business.

How many Reaganists does it take to change a light bulb?
Ten. One to deny that the bulb is burned out, one to clarify the denial ('The bulb is really just dim'), one to blame the bulb burning out on the Carter administration, one to blame the bulb burning out on Congress, one to ask for a Constitutional amendment that will prohibit bulbs from burning out, one to replace the bulb with a kerosene lamp, one to borrow money from the Japanese to pay for the kerosene, one former Reaganist to lobby his old colleagues for a special favour for the kerosene importer, one to cash the cheque for investing in the kerosene importer, and one to send the bill to the next generation.

How many civil servants does it take to change a light bulb?
Forty-five. One to change the bulb, and 44 to do the paper-work.

How many Trotskyists does it take to change a light bulb?
It's no use trying to change it, it's got to be smashed.

How many Communists does it take to change a light bulb?
Two. One to change it, and a second to hand out leaflets.

How many Mafia hitmen does it take to change a light bulb ?
Three. One to change it, one to watch and one to shoot the witness.

◎ ◎ ◎

How many movie actresses does it take to change a light bulb?
One, but you should've seen the line outside the producer's hotel room.

How many procrastinators does it take to change a light bulb?
One, but he has to wait until the light is better.

How many pessimists does it take to change a light bulb?
None. And it's a waste of time anyway because the new bulb probably won't work either.

How many Net poets does it take to change a light bulb?

swimming
None, fish are through the of my consciousness,
and edges
I dark
like the
long-lasting bulbs
the bulb be changed again, since they missed.

How many light-bulb jokes does it take to change a light-bulb joke?
Mmm. The probability that a given light-bulb joke will be submitted to the Net in any given week is 0.4, and the probability that it will have changed detectably since the last transmission is 0.2. Hence (assuming independence, which is reasonable since no submitter of a light-bulb joke ever seems to know it has been submitted before, or at least within the last two or three weeks), the probability that it will change in a given week is 0.08. So it takes about 12.5 light-bulb jokes to change a light-bulb joke.

How many consultants does it take to change a light bulb?
'I'll have an estimate for you a week from Monday.'

How many consultants does it take to change a light bulb?

1 How many can you afford?
2 One, but it'll take three weeks to complete the feasibility study and another six to demonstrate proof of concept.
3 Have you thought about rewiring your whole house recently?

How many existentialists does it take to change a light bulb?
Two. One to change it and one to observe how the light bulb itself symbolises a single incandescent beacon of subjective reality in a netherworld of endless absurdity reaching out towards a maudlin cosmos of nothingness.

How many elephants does it take to change a light bulb?
Two, but it has to be a pretty big light bulb.

How many rednecks does it take to screw in a light bulb?
Six. Then they all beat the hell out of it, leave it lying in a dark alley and brag about it in the pub afterwards.

How many rednecks does it take to change a light bulb?
One. It only takes one person to use a hammer.

Do you know how many musicians it takes to change a light bulb?
Five. One to screw in the light bulb and four to stand around and say, 'Man, if I'd had his studio time, I could have done that.'

Do you know how many musicians it takes to change a light bulb?
Five. One to change the bulb and four to get in free because they know the guy who owns the socket.

Tourist: 'Do you know how many Welsh people it takes to change a light bulb?'
Welsh Choir: 'No, but you sing it and we'll hum the tune in moving harmony.'

How many Freudians does it take to change a light bulb?
Two. One to hold the ladder and one to change the penis. Oops, I mean, er, the light bulb.

How many egotists does it take to change a light bulb?
One. He holds on to the light bulb and waits for the world to revolve around him.

How many Holocaust revisionists does it take to screw in a light bulb?
None, they just deny the bulb ever went out in the first place.

How many homophobes does it take to screw in a light bulb?
(Note: first, they can't be sure the socket's feminine, and, second, they'd really rather the bulbs stayed in the closet where they belong.)
Two. One to do it, and one to supply the sterile rubber gloves, because it's possible that a gay touched the bulb before him.

How many gay men does it take to screw in a light bulb?
Three. One to screw in an Art Deco bulb and two to shriek 'Fabulous.'

How many massage parlour attendants does it take to change a light bulb?
Whatever number turns you on, big boy.

How many feminists does it take to change a light bulb?
One hundred. One to change it, and 99 to wring their hands and agonise about how oppressed the socket is.

How many feminists does it take to change a light bulb?
Eleven. One to do it all by herself, and 10 to form a survivors of darkness support group!

How many feminists does it take to screw in a light bulb?
Seven. One to change the light bulb, three to protest the offence committed by the light bulb in regards to the socket, two to secretly wish they were the socket and one to secretly wish she was the light bulb.

How many feminists does it take to change a light bulb?
Two. One to change the bulb and one to write about how it feels.

How many men does it take to change a light bulb?
Only one, but you have to nag him for a fortnight first.

How many men does it take to screw in a light bulb?
Four. One to do the job and three to listen to him brag about the screwing part.

How many New-Agers does it take to change a light bulb?
Ten. One to actually do it and nine to stand around going, 'Hmm, well, I don't really mind who does it. I mean, I could do it, but of course I wouldn't want to impose my will upon anyone else . . .'

How many New-Agers does it take to change a light bulb?
Two. One to change it and one to check the new one for bad psychic auras (and optionally another dozen to perform the dance of the renewal of the light).

How many visitors to an art gallery does it take to screw in a light bulb?
Two. One to do it and one to say, 'Huh! My four-year-old could've done that.'

How many British trades unionists does it take to change a light bulb?
None. They cannot interfere with the light bulb's inalienable right to its labour.

How many gay-rights activists does it take to change a light bulb?
None. The bulb shouldn't have to change for society to accept it.

How many jugglers does it take to change a light bulb?
One, but it takes at least three light bulbs.

How many Essex girls does it take to screw in a light bulb?
None. They only screw in Cortinas.

How many philosophers does it take to change a light bulb?
Hmm. Well, that's an interesting question, isn't it?

How many philosophers does it take to change a light bulb?
Three. One to change it and two to stand around arguing over whether or not the light bulb exists.

How many philosophers does it take to change a light bulb?
Define 'light bulb'.

How many Zen masters does it take to screw in a light bulb?
None. The Universe spins the bulb, and the Zen master stays out of the way.

How many Zen masters does it take to change a light bulb?
A tree in a golden forest.

How many Zen masters does it take to change a light bulb?
Two. One to change the bulb and one not to change it.

How many Zen masters does it take to change a light bulb?
None. Zen masters carry their own light.

How many Zen masters does it take to change a light bulb?
Three. Two to fetch the wood and one to enlighten the novice.

How many Taoists does it take to change a light bulb?
You cannot change a light bulb. By its nature it will go out again.

How many Christian fundamentalists does it take to change a light bulb?
None. The Bible doesn't mention light bulbs.

How many politically correct clergy does it take to change a light bulb?
None. Politically correct clergy do not change light bulbs. They ban light bulb jokes.

How many lawyers does it take to change a light bulb?
How many can you afford?

How many WASP princesses does it take to change a light bulb?
'What? And ruin my nails?'

How many teenage girls does it take to screw in a light bulb?
One, but she'll be on the phone for five hours telling all her friends about it.

How many actors does it take to change a light bulb?
Only one. They don't like to share the spotlight.

How many Hegelians does it take to screw in a light bulb?
Two, of course. One stands at one end of the room and argues that it is dark; the other stands across from him and says that that is impossible. This dialectic creates a synthesis when the bulb gets screwed in.

How many chickens does it take to change a light bulb?
None. They're all far too busy crossing the road.

How many baby boomers does it take to screw in a light bulb?
Ten. Four to talk about how great it is that they've all come together to do this, one to screw it in, one to film it for the news, one to plan a marketing strategy based on it, one to reminisce about mass naked bulb screwings in the '60s, one

to watch reruns of '50s TV shows, and one to play classic rock.

How many Generation Xers does it take to screw in a light bulb?
Two. One to go and shoplift the bulb so there's something to screw in and the other to screw it in for the minimum wage.

How many one-armed people does it take to change a light bulb ?
Only one, as long as they kept the till receipt.

How many mice does it take to screw in a light bulb?
Two, but they have to be really tiny.

How many Dadaists does it take to change a light bulb?
To get to the other side.

How many Lacanians does it take to change a light bulb?
Three. One to do it, one to desire it, and the ignorant Other.

How many dyslexics does it take to bulb a light-change?
Eno.

How many angels can dance on a light bulb?
It depends on the dance step.

In case you didn't already know the warning signs . . . you know it's time to get out of consulting when:

1 You ask the waiter what the restaurant's core competencies are.
2 You decide to reorganise your family into a 'team-based organisation'.
3 You refer to dating as test marketing.
4 You can spell 'paradigm'.
5 You actually know what a paradigm is.
6 You understand your airline's fare structure.
7 You write executive summaries on your love letters.

8 You think that it's actually efficient to write a 10-page paper with six other people you don't know.
9 You believe every company is 'a traditional functional organisation, with promotion based on tenure, but one that needs to change as it is facing ever-increasing competition'.
10 You believe you never have any problems in your life, just 'issues' and 'improvement opportunities'.
11 You know every single piece of clip art in PowerPoint.
12 You explain to your bank manager that you prefer to think of yourself as 'highly leveraged' as opposed to 'in debt'.
13 You can explain the difference between 're-engineering', 'down-sizing', 'right-sizing' and 'firing people's asses'.
14 You actually believe your explanation in number 13.
15 You like both types of sandwiches: ham and turkey.
16 You believe the best tables and graphs take an hour to comprehend.
17 You refer to divorce as 'divestiture'.
18 You insist that you do some more market research before you and your spouse produce another child.
19 Your 'deliverable' for Sunday evening is clean laundry and paid bills.

A woman went to the doctor's office. When the doctor asked her what her problem was, she said that recently her intestines had been producing entirely too much gas. This was a very embarrassing problem and she hoped that the doctor could help her with it. The doctor said he believed he could help her and, excusing himself, went out of the room. When he came back in he was carrying a long pole with a hook on the end. The woman took a look at the pole and screamed, 'Oh, my God, Doctor. What are you going to do with that thing?' The doctor replied, 'I am going to open the window.'

Let's just say that I try to take one day at a time, but sometimes several days attack me at once.

Yesterday, one of my kids asked me what I did during the sexual revolution. I said I was taken prisoner early on and spent the duration doing chores.

According to the latest government statistics, it now costs over $200,000 to raise a child from birth. The second year costs even more.

I'm a light drinker. It gets light, I start drinking.

I drive a Rolls. Well, it's not exactly a Rolls-Royce – it's a Rolls Canardly. It rolls down one hill and can hardly get up the next.

Last night I dreamt that I was eating a giant, fluffy marshmallow. When I woke up, my pillow was gone.

Going shopping is just like sex, only the roles are reversed. The woman is enjoying it, and the man is asking how much longer.

Be sure to try our famous autumn leaves cocktail. First your face turns yellow, then it turns red, then you fall on the floor.

How am I? Well, I'm better than I was, but I'm not so well as I was before I got to be as bad as I am now.

In Washington, D.C., there was an increase in the number of speeding official government vehicles. Therefore an edict went out from on high. It didn't matter who you were, if you were caught speeding in an official vehicle, you would get a ticket. Sometime after this edict went into effect, President Clinton was going to an important appearance in Baltimore. He was way behind schedule, and he told his driver to speed up. The driver told him about the new edict, and refused to speed up. Clinton said, 'Darn it, just pull over here.' He got out, and told his driver to get in the back. He said, 'I'll drive . . . they wouldn't dare give me a ticket.' So, there they go, 110 miles per hour down the turnpike, and there's two motorcycle cops hiding behind a billboard. The car goes roaring by, and the first cop says, 'Holy cow! Did you see that?' The second cop says, 'You stay here, I'll go give him a ticket.' The second cop is gone for a short while and then returns. The first cop says, 'Did you give that guy a ticket?' The second cop says, 'Aw, no. He was too important.' The first cop says, 'Well, who was it?' The second cop says, 'I don't know. I didn't recognise him. But I'll tell you one thing – Clinton was his driver.'

Lessons life has taught me:

1 The easiest way to find something lost around the house is to buy a replacement.
2 Never take life seriously. Nobody gets out alive, anyway.
3 One good turn gets most of the blankets.
4 Sex is like air; it's not important unless you aren't getting any.
5 There are two kinds of pedestrians – the quick and the dead.
6 An unbreakable toy is useful for breaking other toys.
7 If quitters never win, and winners never cheat, then who is the fool who said, 'Quit while you're ahead'?
8 A closed mouth gathers no feet.
9 Health is merely the slowest possible rate at which one can die.
10 It's not hard to meet expenses, they're everywhere.
11 A jury is a group of 12 people who determine which client has the better lawyer.
12 Never lick a gift horse in the mouth.
13 The only difference between a rut and a grave is the depth.
14 Marriage is the triumph of imagination over intelligence. Second marriage is the triumph of hope over experience.
15 Before marriage, a man yearns for the woman he loves. After marriage, the 'y' becomes silent.

16 If you want your spouse to listen and pay strict attention to every word you say, talk in your sleep.

One day Mrs Jones went to have a talk with the minister at the local church. 'Reverend,' she said, 'I have a problem – my husband keeps falling asleep during your sermons. It's very embarrassing. What should I do?'

'I have an idea,' said the minister. 'Why not take this hatpin with you. I will be able to tell when Mr Jones is sleeping, and I will motion to you at those times. When I motion, you give him a good poke in the leg.'

In church the following Sunday, Jones dozed off. Noticing this, the preacher put his plan to work. 'And who made the ultimate sacrifice for you?' he said, nodding to Mrs Jones. 'Jesus!' Jones cried as his wife jabbed him in the leg with the hatpin. 'Yes, you are right, Mr Jones,' said the minister.

Soon, Jones nodded off again. Again, the minister noticed. 'Who is your redeemer?' he asked the congregation, motioning towards Mrs Jones. 'God!' Jones cried out as he was stuck again with the hatpin. 'Right again,' said the minister, smiling.

Before long, Jones again winked off. However, this time the minister did not notice. As he picked up the tempo of his sermon, he made a few motions that Mrs Jones mistook as signals to bayonet her husband with the hatpin. The minister asked, 'And what did Eve say to Adam after she bore him his ninety-ninth son?'

Mrs Jones poked her husband, who yelled, 'You stick that goddamned thing in me one more time and I'll break it off and shove it up your arse.'

A lady awoke one morning and discovered her dog was not moving. She called her vet who asked her to bring the dog in. After a brief examination, the vet pronounced the dog dead.

'Are you sure?' the distraught woman asked. 'He was a great family pet. Isn't there anything else you can do?'

The vet paused for a moment and said, 'Yes, there is one more thing I can do.' He left the room for a moment and came back carrying a large cage with a cat in it. The vet opened the cage door and the cat walked over to the dog. The cat sniffed the dog from head to toe and walked back to the cage.

'Well, that confirms it,' the vet announced. 'Your dog is dead.'

Satisfied that the vet had done everything he possibly could, the woman sighed, 'How much do I owe you?'

'That will be $330,' the vet replied.

'I don't believe it,' screamed the woman. 'What did you do that cost $330?'

'Well,' the vet replied, 'it's $30 for the office visit and $300 for the cat scan.'

A man decides to buy a new telescope for his rifle. He goes to a rifle shop, and asks the clerk to show him a scope. The clerk takes out a scope, and says to the man, 'This scope is so good, you can see my house all the way up on that hill.' The man takes a look through the scope, and starts laughing. 'What's so funny?' asks the clerk. 'I see a naked man and a naked woman running around in the house,' the man replies. The clerk grabs the scope from the man, and looks at his house. Then he hands two bullets to the man and says, 'Here are two bullets. I'll give you this scope for nothing if you take these two bullets, shoot my wife's head off and shoot the guy's dick off.' The man takes another look through the scope, and says, 'You know what? I think I can do that with one shot.'

One evening at the bar, three friends were chatting about their respective professions. They were a doctor, a lawyer and an engineer. After some drinking and many war stories, the group began arguing over which of their professions was first.

The doctor argued, 'In the very beginning, Genesis, Chapter 1, God took a rib from Adam and created Eve. God was a surgeon, so doctors were the first profession.'

The engineer agreed, saying, 'Yes, you're right about God being a surgeon. Before that, however, God created the Earth and the Sun, and the whole Universe out of mere chaos. God was an engineer, so engineers came before doctors.'

The lawyer, smiling quietly, asked, 'And who do you think created the chaos?'

A secretary walked into her boss's office and said, 'I'm afraid I've got some bad news for you.' 'Why do you always have to give me bad news?' the boss complained. 'Tell me some good news for once.' 'All right. Here's some good news,' said the secretary. 'You're not sterile.'

The small group of astronauts and scientists had spent an entire week on the planet Mars. They had met and were able to communicate with the natives long suspected to inhabit the planet, and were trying to compare life and habits on Mars with our own.

'Tell me,' one earth scientist asked his Martian counterpart, 'just how do you reproduce the species here on your planet?'

'I shall be very pleased to demonstrate,' replied the leader of the Martian group, and he called forth a voluptuous Martian beauty with three heads. They then engaged tentacles for a few moments and, almost at once, a small pouch began to form on the female's back. It grew quite rapidly, and within less than a minute it opened up and a bright Martian flower, almost in full bloom, dropped out. Within another minute, the flower bloomed and from it dropped an identical copy of the mother, only much smaller. It began to scamper around almost at once.

The Earthlings, expecting the same question in return, tried to explain how procreation differed on Earth. The confused Martians though were more or less demanding a like demonstration. After a long conference, and with a great deal of discussion, one of the astronauts convinced one of the female scientists to co-operate and appease their hosts. Neither of the pair was too happy with the arrangement, with the large audience gathered around them, but, after all, it was in the interests of not only science, but of interplanetary relations.

While the couple made love, the Martians observed them from every angle possible in total silence. Only when they were finished did their leader speak. 'That certainly was the most unusual thing I've ever seen.' he said. 'But I still don't understand, was the entire process a failure? Nothing happened.'

'It's difficult to say,' replied the Earth scientist. 'We cannot tell at once. Some tests can be run in a month or so, but, even if the male did in fact fertilise the female's egg, the baby will not be born till at least nine months from now.'

'Nine months?' exclaimed the Martian. 'Amazing, simply amazing. But tell us this then, if the Earth offspring will not come forth for quite some time, why were the two of them in such a hurry at the end?'

Two female ostriches were walking across the desert. They looked back and saw two male ostriches following them. One female said to the other, 'We'd better get moving, they are getting closer.' So they started to trot. A while later, upon looking back, the males again were getting closer, so the females decided to gallop. Upon checking again they saw that the male ostriches were getting really close. One of the females then said, 'Let's hide.' So they stuck their heads in the sand.

The males came to a screeching halt. One said to the other, 'Where did they go?'

Have you heard of Randolf the brown-nosed reindeer?
He can run just as fast as Rudolph but can't stop as quickly.

A labourer goes to a job site to ask for work. The foreman says, 'Can you make tea?' The labourer says, 'Yes, I can.' The foreman says, 'Can you drive a fork-lift truck?' The labourer says, 'Why? How big is the kettle?'

A man dies, and his widow contacts the newspaper to put in a obituary. They say it's a dollar a line. She says one line is enough; she just wants to say 'Fred is dead.' A little while later the paper phones her back and says they have made a mistake in charging her, there's a discount on offer, and she can have two lines for the same price. Does she want to add anything? The woman says yes, they can add 'Car for sale.'

A man who smelled like a distillery flopped down on a subway seat next to a priest. The man's tie was stained, his face was plastered with red lipstick and a half-empty bottle of gin was sticking out of his torn coat pocket. He opened his newspaper and began reading. After a few minutes the dishevelled guy turned to the priest and asked, 'Say, Father, what causes arthritis?' 'Mister,' replied the priest, 'it's caused by loose living, being with cheap, wicked women, too much alcohol, and a contempt for your fellow man.' 'Well, I'll be damned,' the drunk muttered, returning to his paper. The priest, thinking about what he had said, nudged the man and apologised. 'I'm very sorry. I didn't mean to come on so strong. How long have you had arthritis?' 'I don't have it, Father. I was just reading in the newspaper that the Pope does.'

Some of the girls were seated on the porch of the clubhouse at the golf course. The locker-room door was partly open and they could not help but notice a nude man, whose head and shoulders were covered by a bath towel.

After studying the body, one of the girls reported that it was not her husband. A second girl looked at the man and said, 'No, it isn't my husband either.' A third girl, a life-of-the-party type, peered at the masculine torso and blurted, 'Why, he's not even a member of the club!'

Psychiatric Hotline:
Welcome to the Psychiatric Hotline.
If you are obsessive-compulsive,
Please press 1 repeatedly.
If you are co-dependent,
Please ask someone to press 2.
If you have multiple personalities,
Please press 3, 4, 5 and 6.
If you are paranoid delusional,
We know who you are and what you want.
Just stay on the line so we can trace the call.
If you are schizophrenic,
Listen carefully . . .
A little voice will tell you which number to press.
If you are manic depressive,
It doesn't matter which number you press.
No one will answer.

A nun and a priest were travelling across the desert and realised halfway across that the camel they were using for transportation was about to die. They set up a makeshift camp, hoping someone would come to their rescue, but to no avail. Soon the camel died. After several days of not being rescued, they agreed that they were not going to be rescued. They prayed a lot, and they discussed their predicament in great depth. Finally, the priest said to the nun, 'You know, Sister, I am about to die, and there's always been one thing I've wanted here on earth – to see a woman naked. Would you mind taking off your clothes so I can look at you?'

The nun thought about his request for several seconds and then agreed to take off her clothes. As she was doing so, she remarked, 'Well, Father, now that I think about it, I've never seen a man naked, either. Would you mind taking off your clothes, too?'

With little hesitation, the priest also stripped. Suddenly the nun exclaimed, 'Father! What is that little thing hanging between your legs?' The priest patiently answered, 'That, my child, is a gift from God. If I were to put it in you, it would create a new life.' 'Well,' responded the nun, 'forget about me. Stick it in the camel.'

One day a nun was fishing and caught a huge fish for supper. A man was walking by and said, 'Wow, what a goddam fish!' The Sister said, 'Sir, you shouldn't talk to me like that: I'm a nun,' and the man said, 'But that's the name of it: a goddam fish.'

Then the Sister took the fish back to the rectory and said, 'Mother Superior, look at the goddamn fish I caught.' The Mother Superior said, 'Sister, you shouldn't talk like that,' and the Sister said, 'But, Mother Superior, that's the name of it: a goddamn fish.' So the Mother Superior said, 'Well, give me the goddamn fish and I'll clean it.'

While she was cleaning the fish the Monsignor walked in and she said, 'Monsignor, look at the goddamn fish that the Sister caught.' The Monsignor said, 'Mother Superior, you shouldn't talk like that,' and the Mother Superior said, 'But that's the name of it: a goddamn fish.' So the Monsignor said, 'Well, give me the goddamn fish and I'll cook it.'

That evening at supper there was a new priest at the table, and he said, 'Wow, what a nice fish'. And the Sister said, 'I caught the goddamn fish.' And Mother Superior said, 'I cleaned the goddamn fish.' And the Monsignor said, 'I cooked the goddamn fish.' And the new priest said, 'I like this fucking place already.'

A man is driving down a deserted stretch of highway, when he notices a sign out of the corner of his eye. It says, SISTERS OF MERCY HOUSE OF PROSTITUTION 10 MILES. He thinks it is just a figment of his imagination and drives on without a second thought. Soon, he sees another sign which says, SISTERS OF MERCY HOUSE OF PROSTITUTION 5 MILES and he realises that these signs are for real. When he drives past a third sign, saying, SISTERS OF MERCY HOUSE OF PROSTITUTION NEXT RIGHT, his curiosity gets the better of him and he pulls into the drive.

On the far side of the parking lot is a sombre stone building with a small sign next to the door reading, SISTERS OF MERCY. He climbs the steps and rings the bell. The door is answered by a nun in a long black habit who asks, 'What may we do for you, my son?' He answers, 'I saw your signs along the highway, and was interested in possibly doing business.'

'Very well, my son. Please follow me.'

He is led through many winding passages and is soon quite disoriented. The nun stops at a closed door, and tells the man, 'Please knock on this door.' He does as he is told and this door is answered by another nun, in a long habit and holding a tin cup. This nun instructs him, 'Please place $50 in the cup, then go through the large wooden door at the end of this hallway.' He gets $50 out of his wallet and places it in the second nun's cup. He trots eagerly down the hall and slips through the door, pulling it shut behind him. As the door locks behind him, he finds himself back in the parking lot, though facing another small sign, which reads: GO IN PEACE, YOU HAVE JUST BEEN SCREWED BY THE SISTERS OF MERCY.

• • •

A guy was lost in the mall at the Washington Monument. He stopped a cop and asked, 'What side is the State Department on?' To which the cop answered, 'Ours, I hope.'

• • •

A three-legged dog walks into a saloon in the Old West. He sidles up to the bar and announces, 'I'm looking for the man who shot my *paw*.'

Sir Edgbert, knight of the realm, was hurrying home on a cold, dark, wet night when, suddenly, his horse suffered a major coronary and died on the spot. All Sir Edgbert could do was collect up what belongings he could and tramp onwards . . .

After staggering for a spell, he decides that he must get alternative transport. Accordingly, he heads for the nearest building which, as luck would have it, is a small farm. He strides up to the door, bangs on it and shouts, 'A horse. A horse. I must have a horse.'

The door opens to reveal a young girl. She looks at Sir Edgbert and says, 'Your pardon, good knight, but my father and brothers are returning from the village on the other side of the forest and will not be back before noon tomorrow. They are riding all our horses.'

Sir Edgbert is saddened by this and says, 'But I must return home immediately. Have you any idea where I may acquire alternative transportation?'

The young girl says, 'I know of no other horses hereabouts, but sometimes my brothers ride our Great Dane dog when the need arises. Would use of that help?'

Sir Edgbert is desperate and says, 'If I must, I must. Show me the animal.'

The young girl leads the way around the back of the farmhouse to a stable. She disappears inside and returns leading an enormous dog which is quite of a size for riding. Unfortunately, the dog has seen better days. Its coat is threadbare, its legs are spindly and it seems to be breathing laboriously.

Sir Edgbert looks at the young girl and says, '*Surely, you wouldn't send a knight out on a dog like this?*'

⊙ ● ⊙

What did the Buddhist say to the hot dog vendor?
'Make me one with everything.'

Jim Finn, the noted biologist, was stumped. He had spent months studying the little green frogs in the Keefo swamp. Despite all efforts at predator control, the population was declining at an alarming rate.

Finn finally went to the chemistry department at his college to see if anyone there might be able to help. Tom looked into the problem and came up with a solution. The little frogs had succumbed to a chemical change in the swamp's water and simply couldn't stay coupled long enough to reproduce. Tom brewed up a new adhesive, made from a dash of this, a toss of that and, most critically, one part sodium. 'You mean . . .?' said Jim. 'Yes,' said Tom. 'They need a mono-sodium glue to mate.'

Punsters deserve to be drawn and quoted.

Show me where Stalin's buried and I'll show you a communist plot.

Show me a famous composer's liquor cabinet and I'll show you Beethoven's Fifth.

Show me the first president's dentures, and I'll show you the George Washington Bridge.

Santa's helpers are subordinate clauses.

A Wyoming rancher had a bull named Caesar who was getting old. So he decided to sell him on the auction market. The only problem was that the nearest railroad was miles away and across a river that hadn't yet been bridged.

Since Caesar had grown somewhat crotchety in his old age the rancher organised a crew of three men whom he sent off with his ranch foreman to lead Caesar to the railroad line. After two days of travel Caesar and the crew arrived at the river near the market town. The tired crew members suggested to their foreman that they be allowed to relax and fish awhile before catching the ferryboat.

'What shall we do with Caesar while you fish?' asked the foreman.

The men replied, 'Oh, he can just graze on this lush grass along the river.'

After a long period of thought the foreman decreed, 'We came to ferry Caesar, not to graze him.'

Picture a chicken and an egg, lying in bed side by side, each smoking a cigarette. Who came first?

There was once a wise man who loved a beautiful maiden, but she lived in a marsh where his car always got stuck and, besides, her father had a gun, so he never did get close enough to tell her of his passion. However, she had a more energetic suitor who purchased amphibious tyres for his car and, when her father was asleep, speedily carried her off. Moral: Treads rush in where wise men fear to fool.

Two Eskimos sitting in a kayak were chilly, but when they lit a fire in the craft it sank, proving once and for all that you can't have your kayak and heat it too.

PUZZLES

Finished files are the result of years of scientific study combined with the experience of many years.
How many f's in this sentence?
See p. 270 for the answer.

What did the 0 say to the 8?
'I like your belt.'

Why is twice 10 the same as twice 11?
Because twice 10 is 20 and twice 11 is 22.

A bus stops and picks up four people. At the next stop it picks up six people and lets three off. At the next stop it picks up two people and lets four off. At the next stop it picks up six people and lets five off. At the next stop it picks up three people and lets three off. How many times did the bus stop?

1 1 was a racehorse.
2 2 was 1 2.
1 1 1 1 race.
2 2 1 1 2.

INVU4URAQT
See p. 270 for the solution.

Punctuate the following sentence for correct sense:
King Charles walked and talked twenty minutes after his head was cut off.
See p. 270 for the answer.

PALINDROMES

Madam
Eve

Madam, I'm Adam.

Madam in Eden, I'm Adam.

Able was I ere I saw Elba.

Draw pupil's lip upward.

Live dirt up a side track carted is a putrid evil.

Rise to vote, sir.
No, it is opposed, art sees trade's opposition.

A man, a plan, a canal – Panama.

Was it a cat I saw?

Sums are not set as a test on Erasmus.

Draw, o coward!

Doc, note, I dissent. A fast never prevents a fatness. I diet on cod.

Rats live on no evil star.

Straw, no, too stupid a fad, I put soot on warts.

Go deliver a dare, vile dog.

A Toyota. Race fast, safe car. A Toyota.

Top step's pup's pet spot.

A FEW PHRASES AND SUCH

A pavlova appetite on a pikelet income

Back of beyond

Best bib and tucker

Better than a poke in the eye with a burnt stick

Chateau cardboard

Do a sideways

Don't get your knickers in a twist

Don't get your tits in a tangle

Flat out like a one-legged arse-kicker

Fucked by the fickle finger of fate

He's a full set of teeth short of the Osmonds

He's got the wrong end of the stick

I feel like pickled shit

It's as useful as an ashtray on a motorbike

It's more than you can shake a stick at

I wouldn't trust him with a dead dog and a piece of string

I wouldn't wear that to the dunny

Just the bee's knees

Kick up bobsidie

Mad as a meataxe

She comes on like wet latex

She'd talk the hind leg off a donkey

She's got a bee in her bonnet

She talks a blue streak

Shit a brick

Talking nineteen to the dozen

The light's out on the front porch / There's a few sheep missing in the upper paddock / He's a few egg whites short of the pav

Two shakes of a lamb's tail

What's the guts?

WHY SO?

1 Night. There's a man reading a book, and he gets sleepier and sleepier until he nods off and drops his book down the side of his bed. He jerks awake, turns off the light and goes to sleep. In the morning he wakes up, turns on the radio and hears that 300 people have died, and he knows that it's his fault. What's happened?

2 A man is driving a silver Mercedes around and around a block. He pulls up outside a hotel and realises he's bankrupt. What's happened?

3 A residential hotel. A man gets up in the morning, sees his wife in bed, kisses her on the cheek, walks out the door, down the corridor, pushes the elevator button, and when the elevator opens he gets in. He lives on the twelfth floor, and as he gets to the sixth the elevator suddenly stops. The man realises his wife is dead. What's happened?

4 The police are called to the scene of a death. All they find in the room, which has no windows and no furniture, is a man hanging from a pipe which spans the top of the room, and a puddle of water on the ground. What's happened?

5 My grandma's odd, she likes kittens but not cats, puppies but not dogs, coffee but not tea, beer but not wine and so on. Can you explain this?

6 There is a man who lives on the twelfth floor of an hotel. Every morning he gets up, walks down the hall and travels 12 storeys to the ground floor, goes to work and,

after work, comes home. On sunny days he gets the lift to the sixth floor and walks up to the twelfth. On rainy days he goes all the way up. However, if someone else is in the elevator at any point on a sunny day he automatically goes to the twelfth floor. Why?

7 You have an unending supply of water. You have a three-litre jug and a five-litre jug. How do you accurately measure four litres? (Note: you can tip water out of the jugs and refill the jugs as you wish.)

8 There is a fox, a dog, a hen and a farmer. The farmer wants to get all of them to the other side of a river in a dinghy, but he can't leave the hen with either the dog or the fox because they will kill it. How does the farmer get them all across?

9 There's a man found in a desert. He has a backpack. There are no footprints anywhere around him. What's happened?

10 A man is found dead in a room. He's killed himself by a shot through the head. Next to him is a cane. On close examination it turns out that there's some sawdust in the rubbish. What's happened?

Answers on page 270-71.

ANSWERS

p. 264
There are five f's in the sentence.

I envy you, for you are a cutie.

King Charles walked and talked; twenty minutes after his head was cut off.

pp. 268-69

1 The man runs a lighthouse. That's also where he lives. He turned out the lighthouse light, a boat crashed into the rocks below and people died.
2 The man has been playing Monopoly.
3 The man's wife is on life-support system and a power cut brought the elevator to a stop and shut her machine off.
4 The man climbed up on a block of ice to hang himself. Now it's melted.
5 She prefers things with double letters in their names.
6 The man is a dwarf. On rainy days he takes an umbrella and by means of the tip of this can push the twelfth-floor button. Otherwise, he can only reach the sixth-floor button. If someone else is in the lift on a sunny day he can get them to push the twelfth-floor button.
7 Fill the five-litre jug, then empty three litres into the three-litre jug. Empty the three-litre jug. Now, pour the two litres remaining in the five-litre jug into the three-

litre jug. Fill the five-litre jug again. Pour one litre out of the five-litre jug into the three-litre jug to fill it up, from two litres to three. There are now four litres left in the five-litre jug.

8 The farmer takes the hen across. He leaves the hen there, on the other side. The farmer returns and picks up the fox. The farmer then drops the fox off and picks up the hen. The farmer returns to the original point of departure and drops the hen off and picks up the dog. He takes the dog to the far side and the returns to get the hen.

9 The man parachuted out of a plane, but the parachute didn't open – hence the backpack.

10 The man was a dwarf who was one of the star attractions of the local circus. The reason for this is that he was the shortest dwarf in the world. However, another dwarf, from another circus, in a fit of jealous pique, entered the dwarf's room when he was away and sanded an inch off his cane. When the dwarf returned and started his usual daily rehearsal with his cane, because of the missing inch he felt taller than he usually felt. He thought with great dismay that this must mean he was growing and so was no longer the shortest dwarf in the world. In a fit of despondency he killed himself.

ACKNOWLEDGEMENTS

Thanks to Elizabeth Adams, Chris Anderton, Gary Baigent, Barbara, Anne Barnett, Bruce Barnett, Elizabeth Barnett, Joanna Barnett, Jonathan Barnett, Julian Barnett, Kezia Barnett, Marjorie Barnett, Richard Barnett, Ryan Barnett, Sarah Barnett, Stephen Barnett, Martin Baynton, Bernice Beachman, Gib Bogle, Christopher Braddock, Matt Brew, Jessica Brines, Alan Brunton, Nicholas Carew, Paul Carew, Stephanie Carew, Hal Chapman, Angie Cuddihy, Brett Cushman, R. Dare, Perry Davies, Rene Den Harder, Douglas, Olivia Dombrovskis, Annie Goldson, Grant, Ross Hamilton, Ken Harrop, Hazel, Denise Hill, Kate Hill, Reuben Hill, Tui Houpata, Welby Ings, Graham Jackson, John, Frances Joseph, Jessica, Bernard Kaiser, Chris Kaiser, Jimmy Keogh, Mike King, David Kisler, Mary Kisler, James Laing, Beverly Lardner-Burke, Alan Loney, Heidi McGowan, Ewen Marjoribanks, Mark, Peter McBurney, Sue McKenzie, Maya, Jason Micheson, John Miles, Shabnam Dew Mobasheri, Shideh Mobasheri, Dave Moore, Olwyn Moore, Tahi Moore, Walter Moore, Brin Nealy, Paul Newfield, Annie Oxborough, Andy Palace, Lynette Papp, Jocelyn Parker, D. Petrie, Tim Phin, Wiremu Puke, Reanin, Claire Robertson, Frank Rogers, Julian Rosenberg, Brian Schaab, Michael Smith, Steve, Tamati, Tame, Margaret Tibbles, Tim, Karina Tohill, Michael Wah, Geoff Walker, Shaun Walters, Barbara Wilkinson, Richard Wolfe, Zeke, Zeno.

Thanks too to Shirley Stoupe, and Ian and Joy Brash, Suzanne and Dave Bucklee, Sandra and Allan Capstick, Jack Parry, Lynne and Mark Wratten.